D0446113

Mahalia Jackson

Young Gospel Singer

Illustrated by Robert Doremus

Mahalia Jackson

Young Gospel Singer

By Montrew Dunham

ALADDIN PAPERBACKS

First Aladdin Paperbacks edition September 1995
Copyright © 1972 by the Bobbs-Merrill Company, Inc.
Aladdin Paperbacks
An imprint of Simon & Schuster Children's Publishing Division
1230 Avenue of the Americas
New York, NY 10020
Printed in the United States of America
10 9 8 7 6 5 4 3 2 1

Library of Congress Cataloging-in-Publication Data
Dunham, Montrew.
Mahalia Jackson : young gospel singer / by Montrew Dunham. — 1st Aladdin
Paperbacks ed.
      p.   cm. — (Childhood of famous Americans)
ISBN 0-689-71786-5
1. Jackson, Mahalia, 1911–1972—Juvenile literature.   2. Gospel musicians—United
States—Biography—Juvenile literature.
[1. Jackson, Mahalia, 1911–1972—Childhood and youth.   2. Singers.
3. Women—Biography.   4. Afro-Americans—Biography.]   I. Title.
II. Series: Childhood of famous Americans series.
ML3930.J2D8   1995
782.25′4′092—dc20
[B]   93-34072

*For Mildred Falls
and
her nieces, Cheryl and Sheila Carter*

In the preparation of this manuscript I spoke with the Reverend Leon Jenkins of the Greater Salem Baptist Church. I received fine cooperation from the Inter-Library Loan System here in the Chicago area in obtaining all the references from periodicals which I used, including material from the Chicago Public Library. I also received biographical material from Columbia Records.

Illustrations

Full pages

Numerous smaller illustrations

Contents

★ # Mahalia Jackson

Young Gospel Singer

Early Days
in New Orleans

ONE SATURDAY Mahalia Jackson skipped down
the dirt road after her ten-year-old brother.
"Peter," she cried, "wait for me."

Peter was on his way to the levee along the
Mississippi River. He stopped and looked back
at his five-year-old sister, playing along after
him. "Hurry up, Haley," he called.

Mahalia didn't really care whether she caught
up with him or not. Mostly she enjoyed skipping along barefooted in the fine dirt. Gradually the dust formed a light brown coating on
her feet, which looked somewhat like a pair of
shoes. As she glanced down at her feet, she

laughed and called to her brother, "Wait for me, Peter. Wait to see my new pair of shoes."

By now Peter was running up the levee. He called back to Mahalia. "What crazy talk! You don't have a new pair of shoes."

Of course, Mahalia knew that she was only pretending. She laughed merrily and once more looked down at her shoes of dust. Right now she was very happy with these shoes.

Mahalia Jackson was born October 26, 1911, on Water Street in New Orleans. Her father, John Andrew Jackson, was pastor of the Mount Moriah Baptist Church in New Orleans. During the week, he worked part-time as a stevedore, helping to load and unload boats at docks along the river, and part-time as a barber.

The Jackson family lived in a little three-room house in a district called the Front of the Town, where blacks lived. Their neighbors included Negroes, Italians, Creoles, and French.

All of them were poor and had to work hard to make a living.

Nearly every weekend when Peter was home from school, he and Mahalia went to the levee along the river to play with other children. Usually while they were there, they gathered driftwood to burn in the kitchen stove, or caught crabs, shrimp, and little alligators to take home for their mother to cook.

Today, after Mahalia quit admiring her make-believe shoes, she ran fast to catch up with Peter on the levee. As she started hurriedly to climb the levee, she stumbled and fell in the soft grass. Then, flat on her back, she looked up at the fluffy white clouds floating peacefully in the blue sky. "Come on, Haley," called Peter, losing his patience. "Please quit fooling around."

Again Mahalia started to climb the levee but lost her footing and rolled back down the grassy bank. She sat up quickly, brushed the blades of grass from her face and hair, and looked down at her feet. Much to her surprise, her new make-believe shoes which she had so much admired were completely gone.

She shrugged her shoulders and arose to her feet. Once more she climbed the levee, this time more carefully than before. Peter already had gone on down to the edge of the river. He was peering into the water, hoping to catch some little critter to take home for his mother to cook for supper that evening.

Mahalia sat down on the levee and looked at the muddy Mississippi River. The water moved slowly but steadily along with its surface shining in the sunlight. Little glimmers of sunlight sparkled on muddy wavelets far out from the levee.

As Mahalia sat on the levee, she could see big boats tied up at the river docks a short distance away. She wondered whether her father was there, working with other men to load and unload the boats. She wondered what they were putting into the boats or taking out of them. Someday she would ask her father more about loading and unloading boats.

Soon she closed her eyes and listened to the sounds of the city. Nearby she could hear the loud toots of boats traveling up and down the river and farther away the shrill whistles of railroad locomotives. In between she could hear soft gentle music coming from nearby streets. Somehow the whole city seemed to be filled with colorful and exciting sounds.

Soon Mahalia jumped to her feet and ran on down to Peter at the edge of the water. There she found him closely watching a small alligator stretched out in the warm sunshine. He pointed to a stick, which Mahalia promptly picked up and handed to him. Then skillfully he raised the stick and brought it down with a crack on the alligator's head. The varmint never knew what hit him.

Peter and Mahalia now started home, with Peter carrying the little alligator. When they reached the house, Mama asked, "What are you bringing home from the river?"

"A little alligator for supper," Peter proudly replied.

That evening the Jackson family had a tasty feast of alligator tail, baked and smothered with onions and herbs. Soon after supper, Peter and Mahalia got ready for bed. The next day would be Sunday, and they would have to get up early to go to the nearby Mount Moriah Baptist Church. Their father would preach there, as he did every Sunday morning.

When Mahalia climbed into bed, she went right to sleep. A couple of hours later, however, she was aroused by sounds and movements around her. After she awakened, she could hear raindrops pattering on the roof. Her mother was bringing buckets and pans to catch dribbles of water leaking through the roof.

Mahalia turned over and raised herself up on her elbow. She peeked out through the soft light coming in from the kitchen and caught a glimpse of her father sitting by the table. She watched him closely as he read his big Bible and made notes on a sheet of paper beside him. Proudly she realized that he was preparing his sermon to deliver at church services the next morning. Somehow just watching him and being close to him made her feel safer when everything was dark and stormy outside.

Suddenly a big cold drop of water splattered on her face, followed by another and another. She sat up quickly and shouted, "Mama! Mama! I'm getting wet from the rain!"

Her mother came running in with a small

washpan to catch the water. "Jump out," she said calmly. "We'll have to move your bed to the other side of the room."

Mahalia jumped out to help her mother push the bed out from under the leak in the roof. Then she climbed back, hoping no more drops would fall on her. "Now go back to sleep and forget the rain," said her mother.

At first Mahalia was too excited to go to sleep quickly again. For a while she lay listening to the steady patter of raindrops falling on the roof and the frequent splatter of water dripping into the buckets and pans. Finally those continuous sounds lulled her to sleep.

When she woke up the next morning, the sun was shining and the rain was over. The water in the buckets and pans was all that was left of the rain. "It's time to get up, Haley," called her mother. "Hurry to get dressed so I can fix your hair before we go to church."

Mahalia dressed quickly and ran to her mother, who started to brush and braid her hair. At first she stood quietly, but soon she began to jerk and flinch. "Quit wriggling," scolded her mother, giving her a little tap on the side of her head.

"I can't help it, Mama," replied Mahalia. "You're making my braids too tight."

Just then Peter pushed open the ragged screen door and called, "I'm going on, Mama."

"No, wait," replied his mother. "Mahalia and I are ready to go, too."

When they reached the church, they found most of the members of the congregation standing outside visiting. Mama walked through the crowd nodding and speaking to her friends. She entered the church and proceeded down the aisle to a front pew. Peter and Mahalia followed and sat in the pew directly in front of her. Papa was already standing up front by the pulpit.

Soon the people came in from outside and the church was completely filled. The room was steaming hot and flies droned in and out the open windows. Mahalia watched her father proudly as he preached his sermon. Beads of sweat rolled down his face as he spoke and waved his arms. Everybody sat quietly and nobody seemed to mind the heat or the flies.

A choir director led the singing during the services, and one of the ladies played the church organ. The members of the congregation always stood while they sang. Mahalia stood along with the others, only she stood on the seat where she could see.

She loved to sing and knew most of the songs well from singing them over and over again. As she sang this Sunday morning, one grown-up person after another stopped singing just to listen to her. Finally she was the only person left singing in the entire church.

At the end of the services, the choir director said to Mahalia's father, "May we have Mahalia sing in the choir?"

In reply, her father smiled and said, "I reckon so, if you want her, but she is a mightly little girl to sing in a choir."

A New Home

ONE MORNING when Mahalia awoke, the hot sunlight already was pouring through her window. She hastily pulled on her dress and ran to the kitchen. "Mama! Mama!" she called on the way. "I'm hungry!"

"Mama didn't get up this morning," said Peter seriously. "She's sick in bed."

Mahalia stopped short and looked at her brother. He was sitting at the kitchen table, eating corn bread and molasses which he had found on the shelves. He stopped eating for a moment to talk with Mahalia.

"What do you mean, Mama's sick in bed?" she

asked. She looked about the room and could hardly believe her brother's words.

"Just what I said," answered Peter. "She was too sick to get up this morning."

Mahalia found the kitchen strange and empty without her mother. "Mama, where are you?" she called, running into her mother's room.

"I'm right here, Haley," answered her mother in a tired voice. "Don't worry, I'll soon be all right again." She lifted her head a little from the pillow and tried to smile. "Go on and get your breakfast," she said. "Peter will help you find something to eat."

Mahalia went back to the kitchen, feeling sad and worried. This was the first time she had ever had to get her own breakfast. She was no longer hungry, but finally reached up to a shelf for a piece of crumbly corn bread.

"Put the bread on a plate," scolded Peter. "You're dropping crumbs all over the floor."

Mahalia meekly put the crumbly corn bread on a plate and placed it on the table. She got out a pitcher of milk and put an empty glass beside her plate. Then she started to pour milk from the pitcher into the glass, but somehow let the pitcher drop to the floor. Fortunately it didn't break, but it splashed milk in all directions on the floor.

Surprised, Mahalia bit her lips to keep from crying. She reached down and grabbed the pitcher, trying to rescue some of the milk. "What's going on out there?" called her mother.

"Haley dropped the milk pitcher and spilled milk all over the floor," answered Peter.

"Yes, but I didn't break the pitcher," added Mahalia, "and I'll wipe up all the milk."

"Wipe up what you can," said Mama, "and I'll clean up the rest when I get well."

Day after day the children hoped to find their mother better, but she grew steadily worse.

Papa had to go to work every day and Peter went to school. Mama's sisters came to visit her and to help out with the work. Mahalia helped these aunts all she could.

Mama's oldest brother, Uncle Porter, also came to visit and to help. He knew more about the family than anybody else, and had helped Mama and her sisters come to New Orleans to live. Mahalia asked him many questions.

Uncle Porter, Mama, and all their brothers and sisters had been born on a cotton plantation. Their father had been a sharecropper on the plantation. He had grown cotton on a patch of ground and received a share of the cotton for his work. All his children had worked with him to help raise the cotton.

Once when Uncle Porter was visiting Mama, Mahalia asked, "Uncle Porter, how did you ever get to New Orleans?"

"That's a long story," replied Uncle Porter,

taking her on his knee. "One time when I was growing up, I got mad at the plantation owner and he got mad at me. I talked mean to him and he talked mean to me."

"Did you have a fight?" asked Mahalia.

"No, but right then and there I made up my mind to leave the plantation," said Uncle Porter. "I got a job in the kitchen on a river boat and learned to be a cook. Then for years I worked as a cook on river boats that traveled south to New Orleans."

"Now tell me about bringing Mama here to New Orleans," begged Mahalia.

"Well, after I got acquainted here, I went back to the plantation to get some of my sisters," replied Uncle Porter.

By now Mama, propped up in bed, listened closely to Uncle Porter's story. Suddenly, Uncle Porter turned to her and asked, "Charity, do you remember how I brought you here?"

"I surely do," replied Mama. "You brought me here on a steamboat. Then you got me a job as a maid at Captain Rucker's house."

"The captain was a good friend of mine," said Uncle Porter. "I made my first trip down the Mississippi River on his steamboat."

"Yes, he really liked you," said Mama. "He used to call you his colored son."

Uncle Porter laughed. "That's right," he said. "He took me into his house and finished raising me just like his own children."

Mahalia sat down on a little stool and listened to her mother and uncle talk of their early years in the country and their first years in New Orleans. She tried to keep quiet because Mama seemed to enjoy talking.

As the days went on, Mama grew weaker and weaker. Everybody wanted to help her, but nobody could do anything to make her better. Finally one day she died.

All the relatives gathered and took Mama by train and boat back to the country neighborhood where she had grown up. They had services for her in the little church which she had attended as a child. Then they buried her in the little cemetery by the church.

At the cemetery, Mahalia looked curiously at her father's dark face, wet with tears. She was too young to fully understand why he and all the others were crying. Somehow she felt that when she returned home, her mother would be there just as she had always been before.

Soon the relatives gathered at the railroad station to return to New Orleans. They talked seriously and softly and stepped over to tell Papa how sorry they felt because Mama had died. Some asked him what he planned to do about Mahalia and Peter. Mahalia felt so lonely that she climbed up on the bench in the station just to be closer to her father.

Soon the railroad train came, and Mahalia's father picked her up and carried her into a coach. Peter and all the relatives followed and sat in seats close by. Before long the relatives began once more to talk among themselves. Mahalia listened closely because she could tell they were talking about her and Peter.

One aunt said, "I would be glad to take them to raise, but I don't have enough room."

Another aunt said, "Possibly one of us can take Peter and another one can take Mahalia. I'll be glad to take Peter, if one of you will take Mahalia."

A third aunt said, "Well, if you will take Peter, I'll be glad to take Mahalia."

Finally a fourth aunt, whom everybody called Aunt Duke, spoke up. She was older than the others and spoke with authority. "Peter and Mahalia should stay together as brother and sister," she said. "I'll take both of them."

Aunt Duke's statement seemed to settle everything. All the others, including Papa, agreed that this offer which she had made would be best for the children. Aunt Duke was a dark brown-skinned woman with a firm, determined look in her eyes. Often Mahalia felt as if she was looking straight through her.

Within a few days Peter and Mahalia moved in with Aunt Duke and Uncle Emanuel, wondering what their new life would be like. Both knew, however, that they had no other choice.

A Busy Day
for Mahalia

"HALEY! HALEY!" called Aunt Duke one summer morning. "Get out of bed and come to breakfast. Nobody in this house can lie around in bed in the morning. You must do your work early while it's still cool."

Mahalia rolled over, stretched and sighed, and put one foot out on the floor. Living here certainly was different from living back home with Mama. Aunt Duke wouldn't let anyone stay in bed past sunrise.

When Mahalia reached the kitchen, she took her place at the table with Peter and Uncle Emanuel. Aunt Duke, dressed in the blue uniform which she would wear at work, stood waiting by the stove. Quickly she placed two fried eggs and a piece of fresh hot cornbread on Mahalia's plate. Uncle Emanuel handed Mahalia a pitcher of brown molasses to pour on her cornbread. Peter was busy eating, because he was working as a yard boy during the summer.

Before Aunt Duke left her work, she gave Mahalia strict orders of things to do during the day. "First, wash and wipe the kitchen dishes and put them away," she said. "Then scrub the kitchen floor and be sure to clean all the corners. Afterwards go down the street and get a big bag of Spanish moss, so we can stuff a bed mattress when I get home."

After Aunt Duke left, Mahalia, Peter, and Uncle Emanuel continued to sit and talk. Peter told about the work he would have to do as a yard boy during the day. "It won't be long before school will begin again," he said. "Then

I won't have a chance to work during the day to earn money."

"Yes, this fall I'll be old enough to start to school," chimed in Mahalia. "I can hardly wait to learn to read."

"You're smart and I'm sure you will learn real fast," said Peter, leaving the house to start his day's work.

Now only Uncle Emanuel and Mahalia were left at the table. "I still have time to work in the garden a while before I need to leave," he said. "How would you like to come out to help me after you finish doing the dishes?"

"Oh, good!" cried Mahalia. "That will be fun. I'll be out to help you."

Carefully she scraped the sticky molasses from the plates and stacked them on the table. She placed a big tin dishpan in the sink for washing the dishes and got out a smaller pan for rinsing them. She brought a kettle of hot water from the top of the cookstove and poured some of it into the dishpan and the rinsing pan. Then she reached up to the handle of the pump at the end of the sink and pumped cold water into the dishpan.

She stirred the water round and round with her fingertips to mix the cold water with the hot water. She took down a bar of homemade soap and swished it about in the water to make it sudsy. Finally, one by one, she washed the dirty dishes in the soapy water and rinsed them in the pan of hot clear water. Then she wiped each one dry with a clean cloth.

After she had put away all the dishes, she carried the small pan of rinsing water and emptied it out the back door. Next she picked up the big dishpan of soapy water and started for the door. This dishpan was so full, however, that she slopped soapy water all over the front of her dress. By the time she reached the door, her dress was soaking wet, but she was too happy to care. She just looked at herself and laughed. Moments later she ran from the house to the garden and called, "Here I am, Uncle Emanuel, ready to help."

"Good," cried Uncle Emanuel. "You may pull weeds along the row of beans over there at the side of the garden."

Mahalia ran to one end of the row and started to work. Already she had learned that in weeding, she should grab a weed next to the ground and try to pull it out by the roots. Carefully she pulled the weeds and threw them on the ground in the hot sun to wither and die.

As the rays from the sun became hotter and hotter, Mahalia began to suffer from the heat, but she kept right on pulling weeds. She looked over and could see sweat rolling down Uncle Emanuel's dark cheeks, but he kept singing contentedly as he worked.

Mahalia eagerly looked toward the end of the row. At last she pulled the last weed and threw it to the ground. "There, Uncle Emanuel," she called. "I have finished my row."

Uncle Emanuel came right over to look at the row, which she had weeded. "You surely have done a fine job, Haley," he said, "just as good as I could have done. Now go on into the house out of the hot sun."

Uncle Emanuel rubbed his face and neck with a big red handkerchief. He stood for a moment to admire the neat healthy rows of corn, tomatoes, beans, okra, mustard greens, and cabbage growing in his garden. "This is a good place to live," he said, almost to himself. "From this garden we get all the vegetables that we need. From the river we get all the fish, crabs, and shrimp that we need."

"And we have Aunt Duke to bake good cakes and pies," added Mahalia.

Uncle Emanuel laughed and agreed. "Yes, Aunt Duke is a mighty fine cook," he said. "You're a good little weed puller, and someday I predict you'll be a mighty fine cook, too."

Mahalia was happy with these words. She watched Uncle Emanuel as he walked down the street. Before long he turned and waved at her, and she waved back at him. Already, she felt lonely at home by herself.

As she walked slowly toward the house she noticed her old rag doll resting on the back step. "Oh, Debra Sue!" she cried, reaching over to pick her up.

This doll was homemade with black buttons sewed on her head for eyes. Her hair was made of grass held in place by a sock pulled over her head for a cap. When Mahalia picked up the doll, she noticed that her hair was brown and withered. "Your hair is dried out," she said. "I'll have to get you some new hair."

She plucked tall blades of green grass and started to make a braid for the doll. When she had almost finished the braid, she noticed the other end of it had started to unravel. "Oh," she exclaimed, "now this braid is ruined, and I must make another one."

She plucked some more grass and looked around for a flat stone to place on one end of it to keep it from unraveling. Then she got down on her knees and braided the grass neatly without having any more trouble. She held her mouth tightly and grimly as she worked.

When she finished the braid, she removed the sock and old braid from the doll's head. Carefully she replaced it with the new braid which she had just finished and pulled on the sock to keep it in place. Finally she held up the doll to admire her new hair and started to rock her gently back and forth.

Suddenly she remembered that Aunt Duke

had ordered her to scrub the kitchen floor. She jumped up and leaned the doll against the back step. "Now, Debra Sue, take a little nap while I do my work," she said. "I'll be back in a little while."

She ran into the house, poured some lye in a bucket of water, and got out a big scrub brush. Moments later she dropped to her knees and started to scrub. Her hands smarted from the lye in the water, but she kept right on swinging the brush over the floor.

She remembered that Aunt Duke had told her to scrub all the dark corners, so she scrubbed them first. Last, she scrubbed the center of the floor which she could see clearly from sunlight shining in through the screen door. As she scrubbed, she kept backing up on her knees. Finally, when her feet touched the screen door, she knew that she was almost done.

Quickly she jumped to her feet, emptied the

water out the back door, and put away the bucket and brush. Eagerly she started out the back door to play with Debra Sue again. Just at that moment Aunt Duke called to her from the front door, "Haley, have you brought home the moss? I have come home early to fill the mattress."

At this question, Mahalia's heart almost leaped into her mouth. "No, but I'll go after it right now," she replied meekly.

Aunt Duke's face had an angry look. She went to a closet and pulled out a big basket. "Here, take this basket and bring it back completely filled," she said in a scolding tone.

Mahalia rushed down the street, carrying the big basket. She had pulled moss from the branches of gnarled old trees before and looked forward to the fun she would have. Soon she heard someone calling to her from one of the houses, "Haley, where are you going?"

She stopped to look and saw an Italian neighbor boy, Gino, sitting on his front step. "I'm going to get moss," she answered.

"May I go, too?" asked Gino.

"Sure," replied Mahalia. "You can help me gather some of the moss."

Soon Mahalia and Gino came to a long row of gnarled oak trees with long bunches of Spanish moss hanging from their branches. Mahalia looked up and hardly knew where to begin picking. She pulled down several bunches and stuffed them into the basket.

Gino, close beside her, also started to pull down bunches of moss. Once he pulled extra hard on a bunch and when it came loose, he fell backward on the ground, covered with moss. Mahalia looked down at him and laughed.

Before long Mahalia swung herself up to the first limb of a tree and started to pull bunches of moss from higher limbs and drop them to the

ground. She climbed higher and higher in the tree. Down below Gino picked up the bunches of moss and put them into the basket.

Finally Mahalia, standing on a limb, paused to rest against the trunk of the tree. She was fascinated by the beauty of the sunlit branches, draped with shimmering, gray-green moss. A gentle breeze fanned her face, and she felt joyful and happy. "Come on down," called Gino down below. "What are you doing?"

"I'm just resting and enjoying myself," replied Mahalia. "Everything is so beautiful up here I don't want to come down."

"Well, come on," he replied. "We have all the moss we can carry."

Mahalia and Gino started home with the heavy basket, one holding the handle on one side and the other on the other side. Soon Mahalia said, "Wait a minute, let's change sides. The handle is cutting my hand."

"Quit fooling," said Gino. "You just want an excuse to rest."

"Hush, Gino," exclaimed Mahalia. "That's not so. Come on, let's go."

Gino helped carry the heavy basket of moss to the back door of the house. Mahalia pulled open the door and dragged the basket on into the house. "Here's your basket of moss, Aunt Duke," she called.

Aunt Duke was waiting with all the materials which they would need for making and stuffing a mattress. She had several old cotton cement sacks which they would sew together to make a mattress cover. She had a bag of corn husks, which they would use along with the Spanish moss for stuffing the mattress.

Mahalia stood quietly while Aunt Duke pushed a twine cord through the eye of a long needle and tied a knot at the end of the cord. She handed the threaded needle to Mahalia and picked up another needle which she had already threaded for herself. Then the two of them started to stitch together the old cotton sacks to make a mattress cover.

Aunt Duke pushed her needle in and out of the cloth quickly and easily. Mahalia, on the other hand, pushed hers in and out of the cloth slowly and awkwardly. She wondered how Aunt Duke could sew so swiftly, but finally she managed to finish a seam. Aunt Duke carefully inspected it and half-smiled in approval.

Now the new mattress was ready to fill with corn husks and Spanish moss. Aunt Duke held one end open while Mahalia dumped in first an armful of corn husks and then an armful of moss. "Push them into the mattress as far as you can reach," said Aunt Duke. "We must stuff it as full as possible."

Mahalia shoved the corn husks and moss in as far as she could reach with her short arms. Before long Aunt Duke held up the mattress and shook the corn husks and moss toward the bottom. Then Mahalia stuffed as much more of the corn husks and moss as she could, and Aunt Mahalis stuffed in still more. At last Aunt Duke sewed up the open end of the mattress and the job was done.

Mahalia looked curiously at the new plump mattress. "Climb on it and see how soft it feels," said Aunt Duke.

Joyfully Mahalia jumped on the mattress and started to bounce up and down. She felt so happy that she giggled with every bounce.

A Trip
to the Levee

IN THE FALL after Mahalia went to live with Aunt Duke, she started to school. Each weekday she walked to and from school with Peter and a few neighbor children. She thought that going to school was important because now she could learn to read.

Her closest friend at school was a girl of the same age, named Sally Lou. One afternoon, when they returned home from school, Sally Lou asked Mahalia to go to the levee with her. "May I go to the levee with Sally Lou?" Mahalia called to Aunt Duke.

"Yes, but don't stay very long," answered

Aunt Duke. "I'll expect you back home by the time the sun sets, or a little before."

The two girls ran on, but Aunt Duke called extra orders to Mahalia. "Take a bag with you to fill with pieces of driftwood," she said. "I need wood for the stove."

Mahalia ran back and Aunt Duke handed her a big burlap bag for carrying the wood. Sally Lou ran home to get a burlap bag so she could bring home some crabs or shrimp for her mother to cook. Then both girls skipped on toward the levee to have fun.

When they reached the levee, they climbed to the top to look up and down the river. They watched steamboats with paddlewheels stirring up the water and leaving dripping spray behind them. They saw other steamboats tied up at nearby docks, where stevedores were busy loading and unloading them.

Sally Lou was first to go down to the edge of

the water. She pulled a small bucket from her burlap bag and started to scoop up crabs which she could see crawling about. Time after time she scooped up crabs and poured them into the burlap bag.

A few minutes later Mahalia began to look for pieces of driftwood. Soon she noticed several pieces floating a few feet out in the water. She picked up a pole and tried to pull the floating pieces toward her.

The pole was too short to reach the pieces of wood, so she stepped out into the water. Her feet sank deep in the soft, oozy mud, but she managed to pull the pieces of wood from the river. Then she used the pole to help push herself back out of the mud.

Cautiously she carried the wet pieces of wood to the top of the levee and spread them out to dry. Finally she wiped her muddy hands and feet in the nearby grass and sat down to rest.

Gradually her thoughts turned to herself. She wondered whether she always would live in New Orleans, or whether she would live some-place else. She hoped that she wouldn't have to grow up just to do housework. Now that she was going to school, maybe she could learn to do other things, too.

Soon she rolled over on her stomach and stretched out with her upturned hands support-ing her chin. As she lay gazing at the water, she thought of God and felt that He would make a place for her. She only wished that she knew what this place would be.

The great orange sun slipped down slowly in the west until it left only a golden streak across the river. Mahalia arose and started to put the pieces of firewood into her burlap bag. At once Sally Lou joined her and the two girls took off with their two loaded bags.

When they almost reached home, they could

hear jazz music coming from a dance hall down the street. Even though Mahalia was dragging a bag of heavy firewood, she started to keep time to the rhythm of the music. She often had wished that she could go down the street to peek into the dance hall, but she knew that Aunt Duke wouldn't let her.

Aunt Duke was standing in the door watching for the girls to return home. When she caught a glimpse of Mahalia swinging along under the spell of the jazz music, she was extremely angry. "Haley!" she shouted. "Get on inside the house where you belong."

Dutifully Mahalia walked into the house, dragging the bag of heavy firewood. She still could hear the lively music and could scarcely keep from dancing. "Is that wood dry?" asked Aunt Duke, breaking the spell.

Mahalia reached her hand into the bag and felt the wood. "No, it isn't Aunt Duke," she

53

replied. "I spread it out on the levee for a while to dry in the sun, but it is still wet."

"Then put it outside by the back step to dry," ordered Aunt Duke.

Slowly Mahalia carried the wood outside and leaned it against the house. Once more she paused to listen to the swinging jazz music coming from the dance hall. Aunt Duke looked out, shook her head, and sighed. "All right," she said, "you may sit here on the step and listen, but don't you dare to leave."

Mahalia sat down on the top step while the darkness of night gathered around her. She didn't notice the darkness because she was charmed by the blaring music. She just sat and listened, contented and happy.

Before long, she began to hear music coming from the Sanctified Church next door. She listened closely as the members of the congregation began to sing, "I'm So Glad Jesus Lifted Me

Up." Besides the singing, she could hear drums, cymbals, and tambourines gloriously beating out the rhythm. Soon this beautiful music completely drowned out the blaring jazz music coming from the dance hall.

Through the open windows of the church, Mahalia could see the shadows of the members of the congregation as they started to clap their hands and stamp their feet while they sang. Soon she rose to her feet and began to sing, clap her hands, and stomp her feet along with the others. Aunt Duke came to the door and smiled happily as she watched and listened.

From Church to Sugar Mill

ONE FRIDAY morning in summer while Mahalia was on vacation from school, she ran happily to the Mount Moriah Baptist Church. Each Friday forenoon she and other children cleaned the church to get it ready for the weekend services. In return for their help, they were allowed to take turns ringing the bell for the Sunday morning services.

When Mahalia entered the church, one of the church women greeted her and handed her a big dust rag. "Good morning, Haley," she said. "I have an important job for you today. You may take this rag and dust the furniture."

This was a big task, but Mahalia didn't object. She took the rag and started carefully to wipe off the pews. As she worked, she figured out where she and Aunt Duke usually sat and where other church people usually sat. She thought of the different kinds of services which were held in the church.

When she finished dusting the pews, she went up front to dust the altar. She moved timidly because she realized that this was a sacred place to kneel and pray. Often members of the congregation gathered here to pray, and sometimes sinners came in from the streets to seek forgiveness from their sins.

Only a few evenings before, a pretty young woman from the dance hall down the street had come to the weekly prayer meeting. She wore fancy store-bought clothes and had sat in one of the back pews. About midway of the meeting, she had jumped to her feet and started to

57

shout and scream. Then she had marched to the altar, dropped on her knees, and prayed God to help her mend her ways.

After Mahalia finished dusting the altar, she stepped up to the pulpit. To her this pulpit was an important part of the church. It was important because her own father stood here each Sunday to preach the gospel.

Finally she left the pulpit and moved over to the organ, which also seemed important because she loved church music. First she wiped off the stool which stood in front of the organ. Afterwards she sat on the stool to dust the front of the organ and the keys.

She took a corner of the cloth and polished all the keys on the organ, one after another. Each time she pushed down a key to polish it, it popped back up without giving out a sound. All the while she sat dusting she wished that she could run her fingers over the keys to make them play music. Even though she didn't know how to play the organ, nothing could keep her from singing. Suddenly she whirled herself around on the organ stool and started to sing one of her favorite songs. The church woman who was in charge of cleaning the church stood by and laughed. "I declare," she exclaimed, "you surely do love to sing."

She came over to inspect Haley's dusting. She wiped her fingers over different pieces of furniture but couldn't find any dust. "All right, Haley, you've done a fine job of dusting. For being so careful you may ring the church bell Sunday morning."

"Oh, thank you!" cried Mahalia. She was so happy that she jumped from the stool and started to run home to tell Aunt Duke.

At home Aunt Duke was in no mood to listen to Mahalia. Instead she handed her a basket and said, "Here, take this basket and go over to the railroad tracks to pick up some lumps of coal for the kitchen stove."

Mahalia took the basket and started skipping down the road toward the railroad tracks. A few houses away, she found her friend Sally Lou, swinging on the gate in front of her house. "Hello there, Haley," called Sally Lou. "Where are you going with that basket?"

"I'm going to the railroad tracks to pick up some chunks of coal for Aunt Duke," replied Mahalia. "Do you want to go along?"

Just then Sally Lou's mother looked out and saw her swinging on the gate. "Stop riding on that gate," she shouted angrily. "Get off before you break it down."

"All right, Mama," answered Sally Lou. "I'm going over to the railroad tracks with Haley." She jumped off the gate and ran into the road to go along with Mahalia.

The two girls skipped along together. When

they reached the railroad tracks, they started to pick up small lumps of coal which had fallen off railroad cars loaded with coal. First one and then the other put small lumps of coal into the basket. Before long Sally Lou called, "Stand back from the tracks, Haley. A train is coming toward us."

There were many railroad tracks here side by side. They were part of a railroad yard where switch engines pulled cars to and from nearby factories and to docks along the river, some to be loaded and some to be unloaded. Mahalia looked up and saw a switch engine coming a short distance away. She dragged the basket off to one side on the grass.

The girls stood back from the tracks to watch the train go by. Soon the engine passed, belching out gray-blue smoke that trailed back over the cars which it pulled. The engineer waved at the girls and they waved back.

Now the girls eagerly waited for the caboose of the train to come by. They knew that friendly trainmen sometimes invited children to take rides to nearby factories. There the children could pick up juicy sticks of sugar cane to suck and chew.

Soon the slow-moving caboose came, and the girls could see other children riding inside. A friendly trainman called and invited them to jump on. They ran quickly to the caboose and he helped them up the steps.

At first the girls were sorry they had climbed aboard. There was no room for them to ride inside the caboose, so they had to stand on the rear platform and hold on to some iron crossbars. Every now and then they had to close their eyes for protection from dirty smoke coming from the engine.

When the train reached the sugar factory, the two girls ran to a big stack of sugar cane. They looked about the stack to find stalks still filled with sweet juice. Finally they sat down at the edge of the stack to suck on a couple of sugar cane stalks.

Repeatedly they filled their mouths with sweet juice. Then they started to chew the sweet pulp inside the stalk. All the other children sat or stood nearby, sucking and chewing stalks of sugar cane.

Before long, the train was ready to start back up the track. "All aboard," called the friendly trainman, and all the children climbed onto the caboose. Mahalia and Sally Lou stood on the back platform again, each trying to hold on to an armful of sugar cane.

When the time came to get off, they jumped from the slow-moving caboose. Sally Lou managed to land on her feet, but Mahalia stumbled and fell. She went rolling down the bank, holding tightly to her armful of sugar cane stalks.

Quickly she climbed to her feet and joined Sally Lou to start walking home. The two girls sauntered along leisurely, munching the sweet pulp from the sugar cane stalks. Suddenly Gino and his friend Joe appeared and tried to take the sugar cane stalks away from them.

Both girls started to fight. Mahalia flung her fists at Gino and grabbed him around the neck. She held him so tightly that he could scarcely breathe. "Please let me go," he begged. "You're choking me."

"All right," she said, "but don't ever try anything like this again!" She pushed him and sent him rolling back on the ground.

Just then Joe, who had been fighting close by with Sally Lou, came over and threatened to hit her. She grabbed a stick of wood from the ground and shouted, "Now run as fast as you can before I give you a good beating!"

Joe took one look at Mahalia's angry face and

started to run down the street. The fight now was over and Mahalia rushed over to Sally Lou, who was sitting exhausted under a tree. "Are you feeling all right?" she asked.

"I guess so," replied Sally Lou, "but I'm certainly mad at those boys."

"So am I," said Mahalia. "If they want some sugar cane stalks, they should go after them just as we did."

Just as the girls were ready to start on, Sally Lou noticed a big torn place in Mahalia's dress. "Oh, my," she exclaimed, "you have a tear in your dress."

Mahalia looked down and saw a big tear near the bottom hem of her dress. "Now I'll really catch it when I reach home," she said.

The two girls stood for a few minutes, chewing pulp from sugar cane stalks. When they started on again, Mahalia said, "I think I'll stop at the barber shop to see Papa."

Mahalia liked her father and tried to see him as often as possible. She saw him every Sunday morning when he preached at the Mount Moriah Baptist Church, and during the week whenever she could at the barbershop. He worked there late each afternoon and evening.

When they reached the barber shop, Sally Lou ran on home and Mahalia stepped inside. "Hello there, Chocolate Drop," called her father as he glanced at her torn dress. "What happened to you?"

"Sally Lou and I just had a fight with Gino and Joe," she explained. "They tried to take sugar cane stalks away from us which we had brought from the sugar mill. Usually they're good friends, but now we're mad at them."

Papa merely smiled and went on cutting hair. Mahalia sat down in a nearby chair and told him all about her train ride to and from the sugar cane factory. Finally she jumped up and said, "I guess I'd better go on home now. Aunt Duke will be looking for me."

Her father stopped cutting hair and came over to kiss her good-by. He handed her a carefully folded one-dollar bill and told her to give it to Aunt Duke. He tried to give Aunt Duke as much money as he could to help pay her for keeping Mahalia and Peter.

The moment Mahalia walked into the house, Aunt Duke noticed the tear in her dress. "How did that happen?" she demanded angrily. Then without hesitating, she went right on to ask, "And where is the basket of coal?"

Mahalia was stunned. In all the excitement she had completely forgotten about the basket of coal. "It's down by the railroad track, Aunt Duke," she replied. "I'll go back to get it and bring it as quickly as I can."

She ran from the house and kept on running until she came to the place where she had boarded the caboose. All the way she kept wondering what she would do if someone had stolen the basket of coal. Fortunately, when she arrived she found it right where she had left it.

On the way home, she held the basket in front of her and got black coal dust all over her torn dress. When she reached the house, she took the basket to the back door and called, "Here is your basket of coal, Aunt Duke."

Aunt Duke looked at Mahalia's torn and dirty dress and muttered, "Humph!" but asked no further questions. Instead she pointed to the kitchen table and added, "Sit down and eat supper. Then take your bath and go to bed, so you'll be ready to go to church early tomorrow."

Friday evening always was a busy time at Aunt Duke's house. All the cooking had to be done for the weekend, because everybody spent both Saturday and Sunday attending different services at the church. All members of the family had to take baths and lay out their clean clothes. Then on Saturday morning they had to get up early and take off for church.

Mahalia liked going to church for the weekend services. She hummed a tune as she took her bath and grinned as she watched Aunt Duke get out a clean dress for her to wear the next day. Finally she went to sleep, thinking of the fun she would have ringing the church bell on Sunday before Papa started to preach.

A Christmas to Remember

EVERYBODY in New Orleans was getting ready for Christmas. The school which Peter and Mahalia attended had closed for the holidays. Christmas trees and candles could be seen in many windows, and people along the streets could be heard singing Christmas songs.

At last Christmas was only two days away. That night when Mahalia went to bed, she was too excited to sleep. Through the open door, she could see Aunt Duke busy in the kitchen, cooking different goodies for Christmas dinner. Evidently she was baking something in the oven, because every few minutes she bent down to open and close the oven door. Then the odors of luscious foods drifted through the house.

Aunt Duke had been cooking for several days to get everything ready. Ordinarily she wanted Mahalia to help her with the cooking, but at Christmas time she shooed everybody out of the kitchen. At this time of the year she wanted to do everything by herself.

Before long Mahalia closed her eyes and listened to the people singing Christmas songs in the Sanctified Church next door. She wished she could climb out of bed and run over to join them. Finally when they started to sing a familiar song, she sang along with them.

The next day, which was the day before Christmas, was entirely different for Mahalia. Aunt Duke, who now was trying to wind up her cooking, called on Mahalia to bring many things that she needed. All the while, however, she wanted her to stay completely out of the kitchen.

Once she called, "Mahalia, bring me that pan of eggs from the back porch."

Quickly Mahalia brought the pan of eggs and set it on the table. Then slyly she tiptoed over behind Aunt Duke to peek at a steamy pot of rich, creamy shrimp gumbo cooking on the stove. Aunt Duke noticed her and cried sternly, "Haley, get yourself out of the kitchen. Leave before I throw you out."

Aunt Duke kept on barking orders, but insisted on Mahalia staying outside. "Get me some water. Fetch some wood. Bring me some more eggs," she called in rapid succession.

Between errands, Mahalia stood at the kitchen door watching Aunt Duke work. She was thrilled by the way her aunt beat, patted, and stirred different Christmas foods. At last she interrupted her to ask, "When will Uncle Porter get here for Christmas?"

"His train should come sometime late this

afternoon," answered Aunt Duke. "He should arrive in time to go to church tonight."

Mahalia was eager to see Uncle Porter again. She remembered how she had enjoyed seeing him when he had come to see Mama several years before. Now he was a cook on a diner on a railroad train and she hardly ever got to see him. He had to work nearly all the time.

Aunt Duke's son, Cousin Fred, was supposed to come for Christmas, too, but nobody knew when to expect him. He was a big, handsome young man who worked outside the city. Both he and Uncle Porter told interesting stories.

On Christmas Eve there were special services at the Mount Moriah Baptist Church. The church was beautifully decorated with a big Christmas tree up front beside the pulpit. It was covered with small candles that flickered in the dimly lighted room. Larger candles flickered in the windows on both sides of the church.

Mahalia's father preached a powerful sermon on the birth of Christ. He explained that Christ was the Son of God and what His coming had meant to the world. He ended with a prayer in which he thanked God for sending Christ to help us lead better lives.

That evening Mahalia stayed with the congregation instead of taking her place in the choir. She was eager to sing lively songs with a beat, which she was sure the members of the congregation would sing. As she hoped, the organ pumped out joyful Christmas music and the people sang with all the fervor in their hearts. The whole church rang with the singing, clapping of hands, and tapping of feet. Everybody was filled with the spirit of Christmas.

When the Christmas Eve services ended, Mahalia hesitated to leave the church. Sadly she watched persons put out the lights one by one on the Christmas tree and about the church. At last, when the church was competely dark, she started to cry. Somehow she felt as if a glorious experience had slipped away from her, never to be enjoyed again.

All the while Aunt Duke had watched Mahalia closely and noticed how tense she had been. Finally she walked over to her, threw her arms around her, and said, "Come, Haley. We can't stay here any longer. It's time to go home."

Mahalia was touched because Aunt Duke waited for her and tried to cheer her up. Together they walked slowly out of the darkened church toward home. Now and then Mahalia looked back as if hoping to find the church still filled with joyful words and music.

The following morning, which was Christmas, everybody went to church to celebrate again. Once more Mahalia's father preached, and once more she sang happily with the members of the congregation. Much of the time her voice rang out loudly and clearly above the voices of all the others. She clapped her hands and stamped her feet gaily as she joined in singing, "Born in Bethlehem."

After church all the relatives went back to Aunt Duke's for Christmas dinner. In the center of the table there was a roasted raccoon, stuffed with mushy sweet potatoes. Nearby there were platters of roast pork and roast goose. Scattered about there were bowls of shrimp gumbo and tasty vegetables. Out in the kitchen there were several kinds of rich pies and cakes, ready to be served.

At first all the uncles, aunts, and cousins were too busy eating to do much talking. Finally after they slowed down from eating, they began to talk and laugh. Everybody was happy about seeing the others again.

From time to time Mahalia looked over admiringly at Cousin Fred, who wanted to try all the

special foods which his mother had prepared. He wore beautiful clothes and looked more up-to-date than anybody at the table. Every little while he stopped eating to tell something funny he had seen, heard, or done.

Uncle Porter told about some of his experiences as a cook on a dining car. He explained that sometimes he cooked meals for four hundred persons a day riding on the train. "How can you possibly cook for that many persons in such a small kitchen?" asked one of his sisters, shaking her head in doubt.

Uncle Porter threw back his head and laughed. "I wish you could see the fine meals that I prepare in my kitchen," he said. "I know right where everything is and I can cook faster than any of you can cook in your homes."

All the relatives listened closely as Uncle Porter continued to talk. "There's plenty of room to cook on a dining car, if you know how," he said. "The real problem is keeping track of food after you get it cooked."

"What do you mean by that?" asked Aunt Duke curiously.

"Well, when the train hits a stretch of rough track, a pot of gravy may slide off the stove, and a bowl of salad may slide off a shelf, both at the same time," he said. "Then you have to move fast like this to catch them."

He danced about pretending to rescue a pot of gravy and a bowl of salad, just as he would on a dining car, and everybody laughed.

No Business in Show Business

ALL THE WINTER evenings at Aunt Duke's home were about the same. Peter and Mahalia sat at the kitchen table to study their lessons. Uncle Emanuel usually sat in a rocking chair, resting or sleeping, and Aunt Duke sat in another rocking chair, sewing or mending clothes. One evening while all of them were sitting about quietly, they heard someone push open the door and call, "Hey, are you at home?"

Mahalia looked up and saw her father and two strangers standing in the doorway. She jumped up from the table, rushed over to him, and cried, "Oh, Papa! What a surprise!"

Her father stepped forward and held out his arms to embrace her. "Hello, Chocolate Drop," he cried, hugging her tightly.

After exchanging these greetings with Mahalia, he introduced the two strangers as his cousin Jeannette Burnette and her husband, Josie. Aunt Duke promptly invited them to go into the living room to sit down and talk.

Mahalia looked curiously at the fine clothes which Jeannette and Josie were wearing. Jeannette wore a gaudy red dress with matching gloves on her hands and slippers on her feet. Josie wore a striped suit with a white stiff-front shirt and shiny red silk tie. He had a red handkerchief tucked in his front coat pocket and carried a stiff derby hat.

"Who in the world are these people, wearing such fancy clothes?" Mahalia asked herself. Papa had introduced Jeannette as his cousin and Josie as her husband, but she had never known of them before. They must have money in order to wear such fancy clothes.

After everybody was seated in the front room, Aunt Duke said, "Well, this is a surprise. What brings you to New Orleans?"

"We're traveling with Ma Rainey, and will be here for a few days," replied Jeannette.

"Who is Ma Rainey?" asked Aunt Duke.

"She is a famous colored singer," replied Mahalia's father. "People often call her the 'Mama of the Blues.'"

"Yes, she travels about and puts on a show in a tent," explained Jeannette. "We travel with her and put on our act in her show."

Aunt Duke didn't offer any comment, but Mahalia, who sat next to her, heard her say, "Humph!" under her breath. Already she had told Mahalia many times she was very suspicious of show people. She thought they were too frivolous to do any good in the world.

Before long the conversation changed, and nothing more was said about the show. The grownups started to talk about their friends and relatives. Mahalia knew some of the people they mentioned, but not many.

On Sunday morning Jeannette and Josie attended the preaching service at the Mount Moriah Baptist Church. When they entered the church, they sat directly in front of Mahalia and Aunt Duke. Everybody stared at them and wondered who they were.

Jeannette wore a bright green dress covered with fluffy ruffles, and a big swoopy velvet hat decked out with ribbons and feathers. Josie wore a tightly-fitted blue suit with a stiff-front white shirt and black bow tie. On one arm he held his shiny derby hat, as if proud to display it. Odors of rich perfume came from their clothes and spread about the room.

After her father started to preach, Mahalia

kept twisting and turning to see more of Jeannette and Josie's fine clothes. Suddenly Aunt Duke gave her a hard poke in the side, leaned over, and whispered angrily, "Stop gawking at Jeannette and Josie. Sit quietly the way you're supposed to sit in church and listen to your father's preaching."

Mahalia nodded and tried to sit quietly in her seat. She looked at her father and pretended to listen, but actually she kept on thinking about Jeannette and Josie. She wondered what kind of act they put on in Ma Rainey's show. What did they do in their act? Did they sing? Did they dance? Did they play musical instruments? Did they both do the same things?

Soon Mahalia's father concluded his sermon, and the organist played a few bars of "Amazing Grace, How Sweet It Sounds." The members of the congregation rose to their feet and started to sing. Soon they became filled with the spirit of the song and began to clap their hands and stamp their feet to the rhythm.

Mahalia sang with all the joy and ardor in her soul. From time to time she lifted her chin and closed her eyes feelingly. Her voice rang out loudly and clearly above all the other voices in the room.

Jeannette, who stood directly in front of Mahalia, closed her eyes and listened as if trying to absorb the full beauty of the song. Josie shook his head as if he could scarcely believe his ears. After church they exclaimed, "We loved your singing, Haley. Won't you sing another song for us?"

Mahalia was almost overcome with joy by this request. She was always glad to sing for others, but she was especially pleased to have these cousins ask her to sing. "What song do you want me to sing?" she asked.

By this time most of the members of the congregation had walked out the door, and Mahalia's father came over to talk with the group. "This daughter of yours surely has a beautiful voice," exclaimed Josie.

"Yes, Haley has a mighty fine voice," said her father. "I'm mighty proud of her for the way she sings."

"We have just asked her to sing another song for us," explained Jeannette. "Will that be all right with you?"

"Of course," replied Mahalia's father. Then he turned to her and said, "Go ahead and sing another song for them, honey."

"Wait a minute," interrupted Josie. "The organist is still here. Possibly she can play for Mahalia while she sings."

The organist, who was busy gathering up music at the organ, overheard this conversation. Without waiting to be asked, she sat down at the organ and started to play one of Mahalia's favorite songs. Almost immediately when Mahalia heard the familiar strains, she started to sing. At first, she sang softly, but gradually she lifted her head and sang with all the strength and feeling she could command.

Aunt Duke stood near the door of the church, waiting for the others to join her. She was impatient with having to wait, but her eyes filled with tears as she listened to Mahalia sing. She was proud of Mahalia and had come to love her like a daughter.

When the organist approached the end of the song, Josie motioned for her to keep on playing. At once she switched to another song which she knew that Mahalia liked. Mahalia picked up the new song and sang it with as much strength and feeling as she had sung the first song.

The singing went on and on until Mahalia's father said, "We must stop now and let the organist go home to her family."

Jeannette, Josie, and Mahalia's father went home with Aunt Duke for lunch. When they reached home, Aunt Duke asked Mahalia to help her prepare the food in the kitchen. All the others sat around and talked, mostly about Mahalia's singing. Mahalia wanted to stop and listen, but Aunt Duke kept telling her different things to do.

Soon after everybody was seated at the table, Josie said, "Jeannette and I would like to take Haley with us when we leave."

Mahalia's father looked up and shook his head in surprise. "I don't understand," he said. "Why do you want to take her with you?"

"Because of her beautiful voice," promptly replied Josie. "We believe that she belongs in show business. We would want her to put on a singing act in our show. She could even help to sing the blues with Ma Rainey."

Uncle Emanuel spoke up. "This show business is strange to me," he said. "Just what do you and Jeannette do in the show?"

"We put on a comedy act," replied Josie. "We say and do things to make people laugh."

Jeannette went on to explain. "We travel from town to town and put on our show in a big tent. Usually we stay in each town several days and repeat the show several times. We all travel in a crowd with Ma Rainey. She does most of the singing and the rest of us do other things to entertain the crowds."

Mahalia took a deep breath. She was too excited for words. She closed her eyes and tried to imagine what singing in a show would be like. She pictured herself standing in a bright spotlight, singing to a big crowd of people. Then later she could see herself bowing repeatedly as the crowd wildly cheered.

"There is no question that Haley is a marvelous singer in church," said Mahalia's father, "but

90

how do you know that Ma Rainey would want her to sing in her show?"

"We're sure she would," assured Jeannette without a moment of hesitation. "She is certain to want a girl with such unusual talent."

"Even so, Haley still is too young to travel," said her father. "Besides, she's much too young to be in show business."

"We would look after her just as if she were our own child," argued Jeanette. "You wouldn't have to worry about her."

Mahalia's heart was pounding. She wondered what she wanted to do. On the one hand, she knew that she would like to travel and sing to large crowds of people. On the other hand, she was sure that she wouldn't want to leave her good old Aunt Duke and Uncle Emanuel to travel with Jeannette and Josie. Besides, she wouldn't want to wear frilly store-bought clothes, like the clothes they wore all the time.

Once more Josie spoke up. "There's another thing to remember about Mahalia going into show business," he argued. "She'll make good money and have some to send home to you."

Following this remark Aunt Duke's face took on a cold, hard look. Many times she had felt like speaking up, but so far she had remained quiet. Finally Mahalia's father turned to her and asked, "What do you think of the idea of Mahalia going into show business?"

"I think 'No,'" replied Aunt Duke, almost before he had asked the question.

Jeannette looked over at Aunt Duke, surprised and dumfounded. "What did you say?" she asked. "Did I hear you correctly?"

"I said 'No,'" answered Aunt Duke flatly.

Mahalia looked at Aunt Duke. She could tell by the expression on her face that she was determined. Further arguing wouldn't change her mind, but Josie made one last attempt. "You're forgetting your own welfare," he said. "Haley will send you money from her singing."

Aunt Duke just sat straight and stiff in her chair. She shook her head back and forth and answered, "No," one time after another.

Moments later, Jeannette and Josie bade the others good-by and left. Both Aunt Duke and Uncle Emanuel were glad to see them go.

Joy and Sadness

Aunt Duke had a younger sister, Bessie, who was seven years older than Mahalia. She attended school in the same building as Mahalia, and even though she was older, they became very close friends.

One spring when Mahalia was fairly well grown, they obtained jobs of doing housework together before and after school. They were to work for a wealthy family, washing and wiping dishes and helping to look after several small children. Both were happy to have jobs where they could earn money.

On their first morning at work, they scraped

off the breakfast dishes and stacked them neatly by the sink. Afterwards Mahalia washed them in hot sudsy water and placed them in a big pan. Bessie poured hot water over them to rinse off the suds and wiped them one by one with a dry dish towel. Mahalia was surprised by the large number of dishes which the family had used in eating breakfast. "How many persons are there in the family?" she asked.

"I don't know," replied Bessie, "but they surely left a mess of dirty dishes for us to clean up."

"That's what I was thinking," said Mahalia.

Soon Bessie and Mahalia settled down to their routine of working early mornings and late afternoons. One afternoon, when Mahalia returned home, she was surprised to find Cousin Fred sitting in the kitchen with Aunt Duke and Uncle Emanuel. "Hi, there, Haley," he called.

He jumped up from his chair and grabbed

Mahalia and swung her round and round. She was so dumfounded that she scarcely knew what was happening. Aunt Duke and Uncle Emanuel laughed, but offered no explanation.

Soon Mahalia learned that Cousin Fred was planning to live with his parents and had taken a job down at the docks. Early each morning he arose and went to his work of loading and unloading river boats. Each evening he put on his best clothes and went to nearby dance halls and other places of amusement.

Cousin Fred was a handsome young man with neatly cut hair and pearly white teeth. He usually wore a smile on his face and always seemed to be happy. He got along well with people and everybody liked him.

One night Mahalia curiously watched him get ready to go to a dance hall. He stood before a mirror, poured a sweet-smelling oil on his hands, and rubbed it into his hair. Then he combed his hair to make sure it was just so. "There, Haley," he exclaimed. "How does it look?"

He turned from the mirror and danced about the room while he put on a freshly starched shirt. He stopped dancing only long enough to fasten his big silk tie before the mirror. Finally he turned to Mahalia and said, "Honey-babe, I'm going to step out tonight! I'm going to paint up the town."

Aunt Duke looked over sadly and asked him to hush up. She frowned as he started to leave, but he put his arm around her and said, "Good night, Ma. I'll see you later."

Both Aunt Duke and Mahalia worried whenever he left the house in the evening. They knew that he spent most of his time in dance halls, night clubs, and gambling places, but constantly prayed that he would change his ways.

During the summer Cousin Fred purchased a phonograph with dozens of records for playing blues and jazz music. Mahalia became interested in the music and often played the records when Aunt Duke wasn't at home. Nearly every day she hurried up her housework so she could listen to them. She always felt guilty, however, because she knew Aunt Duke wouldn't approve of her listening.

Usually when she played a record, she sat on the floor in front of the phonograph. Sometimes she closed her eyes and absorbed the colorful, rhythmic sounds. At other times she sang along with the music or rocked herself back and forth to keep time.

One of her favorite records was "I Hate to See That Evening Sun Go Down." She played this record so often that she learned both the words and the music. Then she sang the song feelingly whenever she played the record.

Early in the summer, Cousin Fred left as suddenly as he had come. Nobody knew exactly where he had gone, but word trickled back that he had gone to Kansas City. Mahalia found the house very quiet and lonely after he left. She missed talking with him and seeing him around the house. She was sure that Aunt Duke missed him, too, but she never let on.

That summer Mahalia obtained a job of working with Aunt Bell, another sister of Aunt Duke. Aunt Bell was housemaid for a wealthy family in New Orleans. Mahalia helped her do all kinds of work in the house.

Aunt Bell was a very efficient worker. She showed Mahalia how to prepare many tasty foods that Mahalia had never heard of before. She showed her how to make beds to make them look neat and inviting, and how to iron clothes to make them look attractive.

It was the custom in New Orleans for families to share food and clothing with their servants. Each day when Aunt Bell and Mahalia finished

their work, they were allowed to take left-overs from the table home with them. Often they were handed expensive articles of clothing to take home.

Mahalia liked working with Aunt Bell, but she always was eager to return home. She loved to sit at the table and talk with Aunt Duke, Uncle Emanuel, and her brother Peter. This seemed to be the only time of day when they could relax and enjoy being together.

Aunt Duke was a leader in several ladies' clubs in the community. She ran these clubs with an iron hand, just as she ran her own home. Always she took Mahalia along to her club meetings to take notes for her and to help her in many other ways.

Mahalia now was nearly grownup. That fall she entered the eighth grade and spent a busy year in school. The following spring, when she graduated, she realized that her school days were over. Now she must go out and get a full-time job somewhere in the city.

Soon she obtained work as a laundress. She put in ten hours a day and tried hard to do her work well. She was especially happy to feel that she was earning her own living rather than depending on Aunt Duke.

As she washed and ironed, she spent much time wondering about her future. She liked her work, but she wanted to become something more than a laundress. She realized that she didn't have enough schooling to become either a school teacher or a nurse.

At times her mind turned to show business, but she felt that this would be wild and wicked. She thought of the wailing and blaring sounds of the blues and jazz music coming from dance halls and night clubs along the streets. No, the very thought of show business filled her with a sense of wrongdoing that frightened her.

One night after she had gone to bed, she was awakened by unusual sounds coming from the kitchen. She got out of bed slowly and found Aunt Duke crying bitterly and pacing the floor. From the moonlight coming in through the window, she could see that her aunt's dark face was covered with tears.

She had never seen Aunt Duke carry on like this before and wondered what had happened. When she reached the kitchen, she could hear Aunt Duke mumbling something under her breath, but she couldn't understand what she was saying. Finally she called out, "Aunt Duke, what's wrong? What's the trouble?"

Aunt Duke didn't answer. She merely handed Mahalia a crumpled sheet of yellow paper. Mahalia held the crumped sheet in the moonlight coming through the window and could see that it was a telegram. Then she read the sad news that Cousin Fred was dead in Kansas City.

Aunt Duke arranged for Cousin Fred's body to be brought back to New Orleans for burial. Arrangements were made for his funeral services to be held at the Mount Moriah Baptist Church. A long wake was held prior to the services.

Cousin Fred had many friends, both good and bad, in New Orleans. Several bands played soft music on the way from the church to the cemetery. At the cemetery people stood about in groups and listened with bowed heads.

After the burial services, in accordance with the custom in New Orleans, the bands broke loose and played loud blaring music. They marched back along the streets followed by people singing joyfully. The streets rocked with rollicking music, which Cousin Fred would have loved if he could have been there.

Big Move
to Chicago

ABOUT THE TIME Cousin Fred died, there was much talk among Negroes about moving north to live and work in Chicago. Several members of the Mount Moriah Baptist Church moved to Chicago and obtained good paying jobs. Then they reported back to their relatives and friends how much they enjoyed living there.

Uncle Emanuel wanted to move to Chicago, but Aunt Duke wouldn't leave New Orleans. Finally he decided to go on all by himself to work for a while. Shortly after he arrived, he obtained a job as a bricklayer and kept sending money back to Aunt Duke.

Some months later, when Uncle Emanuel came home, he told of many things that Negroes could do in Chicago that they weren't allowed to do in New Orleans. He explained that they could ride in street cars with white people, eat in restaurants with white people, and hold many of the same kinds of jobs as white people. He reported that a few fortunate Negroes even owned and drove automobiles.

A little later Mahalia's father got a job in Chicago, but he didn't stay long. "That city is too big and rough for me," he said. "It's so big that I could get lost and nobody would ever find me. Besides, there are so many gangsters in Chicago that I could readily get robbed or killed. The city is noted for its many killings and crimes. As for me, I'd rather stay right here in old New Orleans."

Two of Aunt Duke's younger sisters, Aunt Hannah and Aunt Alice, moved to Chicago and liked living there. One day they wrote a surprise letter to Mahalia inviting her to come to live with them. They told her about the many jobs that she could find there. Also they explained that she could attend a nursing school there and take training to become a nurse.

Mahalia read the letter several times to make sure that she understood it. She felt elated by the possibility of attending a nursing school to become a nurse. To her, this seemed almost like a dream come true.

Soon her thoughts turned to the gangsters in Chicago, whom her father had mentioned. Would she want to live in a city where she wouldn't feel safe from day to day? Then she concluded that she wouldn't need to feel afraid, because God would protect her.

She wondered how Aunt Duke would feel about her going to Chicago. She took a deep breath and went to the kitchen to discuss the matter. "Aunt Duke," she said bravely, "Aunt Hannah and Aunt Alice have invited me to come live with them in Chicago. May I go?"

Aunt Duke didn't answer but kept on working as if she hadn't heard. She pointed to a bag of sweet potatoes and said, "Get six or eight of those sweet potatoes ready to cook." She paused for a moment and then added, "I don't understand why you want to go to Chicago to live."

Mahalia obediently took six or eight sweet potatoes from the bag and put them into a pan. She pumped a little water over them and washed them carefully to remove the dirt. Then she took them to the kitchen table, peeled them one by one, and got them ready to cook.

After Mahalia finished peeling the potatoes, she decided to try talking with Aunt Duke again. "I want to go to Chicago so I can attend a nursing school," she explained. "Then maybe I can become a nurse in Chicago."

Aunt Duke looked at Mahalia coldly. "Well, you had better forget about all that nursing business and keep your job right here in New Orleans," she said firmly.

Mahalia felt hurt but said nothing. She had hoped that Aunt Duke would approve of her wanting to take training to become a nurse. Even though her aunt objected, she felt that she should make plans to go to Chicago sometime later on her own.

During the coming weeks, she tried to save as much money as she could to help pay her railroad fare to Chicago. Time after time, she counted her money to see how much more she needed to save. That winter, while she was still saving her money, Aunt Hannah came to New Orleans for a visit. While she was there Mahalia decided to go home with her.

Aunt Duke was still opposed to Mahalia going, but she went to the railroad station to see her off. When Mahalia started out to the platform to board the train, Aunt Duke threw her arms tightly around her. "Be careful up there in Chicago," she warned sadly. "Go to church and be a good girl."

"Oh, I will, Aunt Duke," called Mahalia. "Don't worry about me."

For two nights and one day, Aunt Hannah and Mahalia sat in a coach seat on their long train ride to Chicago. They were surrounded by bundles and had a basket of food which Aunt Duke had prepared for them to eat along the way. At first Mahalia was excited about riding on the train. She sat by the window and pointed out interesting things for Aunt Hannah to see.

Before long she closed her eyes and felt strangely afraid of going to Chicago. She wondered whether she was doing the right thing by leaving New Orleans. Already she felt homesick for Aunt Duke and Uncle Emanuel. She would miss going to the Mount Moriah Baptist Church to sing and to hear her father preach. She would miss going to the levee to watch boats on the broad Mississippi River. Her eyes filled with tears and she wished that she could get off the train and head back to Louisiana.

Aunt Hannah looked at her and suspected that she was homesick. She reached in the basket and pulled out a fried chicken leg. "Here, Haley," she said. "Have a piece of chicken."

"Oh, thank you, Aunt Hannah," said Mahalia, taking the piece of chicken. She turned her head so that her aunt wouldn't see the tears in her eyes. From now on she must think only of what she would do in Chicago. Deep down in her heart she was happy about the opportunities she would have there.

Hours later the train ride became boresome, and Mahalia kept asking when they would reach Chicago. By now she was eager to get started on her new life there. Finally Aunt Hannah said, "Well, our trip is almost over. We can begin to gather up our things."

Aunt Hannah started to stack up the bundles to carry from the train. She pulled an old sweater from a shopping bag and handed it to Mahalia. "Here, take this sweater to put on under your coat," she ordered. "You'll find the outside air very cold here in Chicago."

The train sputtered and lurched as it slowed down to enter the station. All the passengers stood in the aisle with grips and packages, waiting to get off. Aunt Hannah and Mahalia inched their way to the end of the car.

When Mahalia stepped into the wintry air on the covered platform outside, she thought that Chicago must be the coldest place in the world. Aunt Hannah led the way along the crowded platform to the station. Mahalia followed as closely as possible, afraid that she might become

112

lost. "We'll go directly to the taxicab stand in front of the station," said Aunt Hannah.

Outside a blizzard-like snowstorm was sweeping through the city. Aunt Hannah didn't seem to mind either the wind or the snow, but Mahalia could scarcely get her breath or see where she

was going. She felt panicky, because she had never expected Chicago to be like this. "Wait, Aunt Hannah!" she called frantically. "I can't keep up with you."

Aunt Hannah stopped for a moment while Mahalia tried to get her breath. Finally with chattering teeth Mahalia managed to ask, "How much farther do we have to go?"

"Only a few steps more," replied Aunt Hannah, starting on again.

Mahalia, shivering with cold, staggered on a few more steps behind Aunt Hannah. When they reached the taxicab stand, they found no taxicabs there. "We'll have to wait until a taxicab drives in," said Aunt Hannah. "Put down your things and rest."

Mahalia gasped for breath and dropped all her bundles. She wiped her face with a handkerchief and, peering through the falling snow, caught her first hazy glimpse of Chicago. Across the street she could see a long row of tall buildings jutting into the sky. Somehow getting this first glimpse of Chicago made her forget the bitter cold. She felt excited and happy from just knowing she was there.

Soon a taxicab came, and Aunt Hannah started to put her bundles inside. Then she stepped to one side and motioned for Mahalia to put her bundles inside. Suddenly as Mahalia reached for her things, she noticed that the driver of the taxicab was a white man. She grabed her aunt's arm and said, "Look at the driver. We can't ride in this cab."

"Go on and get in," ordered Aunt Hannah. "Remember we're in Chicago."

The taxi driver took them over busy streets and boulevards to the apartment building where Aunt Hannah and Aunt Alice lived. Mahalia was dumfounded when she first saw this large brick building with an ornate iron fence in front.

115

She had never imagined that Negroes could live in a fine building like this.

A few days after Mahalia arrived in Chicago, Aunt Hannah became ill, and Mahalia had to go to work. She obtained a job as a laundress on the north side of Chicago. This served as a shock, because it dimmed her hopes of taking training to become a nurse.

Mahalia found the succeeding weeks long and tedious. She had to get up early and take a long ride to work on an elevated train. As she rode this train between tall, dark buildings, she felt as if she were trapped in a prison. Many times she wished she were back in New Orleans beside the broad, lazy Mississippi River.

Gradually as time passed, she became less and less homesick, and began to like Chicago. She found many new friends to take the place of her old friends in New Orleans. Most of these new friends were in the nearby Greater Salem Baptist Church, which she attended regularly with Aunt Hannah and Aunt Alice.

After the preacher and choir director heard Mahalia sing with the congregation, they invited her to sing in the choir. During the first practice session, the choir director had the members sing, "Hand Me Down a Silver Trumpet, Gabriel." Mahalia sang this song with her usual strength and fervor, and completely forgot she was singing with others.

Suddenly the choir director held up his baton to stop the singing. Mahalia felt sure that he was displeased with her for singing so loudly. Now he might criticize her in front of the other members or even throw her out of the choir. She trembled with fear and wished she could sink through the floor.

Immediately the choir director asked her to come forward. Now she was certain that he intended to punish her in some way or other.

Instead he smiled and said, "You have a beautiful voice and I would like to hear you sing that song again all by yourself."

Mahalia was still nervous but felt greatly relieved. She clasped her hands tightly in front of her and prayed for God's help in singing. Then after the organist finished playing the introduction, she started to sing.

At first she held down her voice and sang softly, but gradually gained confidence and sang with more and more vigor. Finally she threw back her head, closed her eyes, and sang with full might from her soul.

When she finished singing, all the members of the choir were astonished. The choir director walked briskly over to her and said, "I congratulate you, Miss Jackson. From now on you will be a soloist in our choir."

The members of the choir now came forward and crowded around her. One after another, they congratulated her on her singing and promotion. One member said, "Your singing surely brings forth the glory of the Lord."

When Mahalia left the church, she felt elated over being treated so warmly by the choir director and choir members. From this time on, she looked upon the Greater Salem Baptist Church as a haven of happiness in Chicago. Day after day she tried to spend as much time there as she could.

Starting a
Singing Career

WEEK AFTER WEEK and month after month, Mahalia kept on working as a laundress on the north side of Chicago. She willingly worked hard to help her aunts with their living expenses, but still hoped sometime to attend a nursing school. She felt certain that God would help her to do important work in the world.

Each week day she arose before daylight to ride the elevated train to work. After she arrived, she stood continuously by a tub, scrubbing dirty pieces of laundry, or by an ironing board, flattening out wrinkles or putting in creases. By evening she was so exhausted that she could scarcely drag her feet up the stairway to take the elevated train home. She always had to stand on the train, because it was too crowded for her to find an empty seat.

Even though her train ride home was uncomfortable, she usually found it relaxing. Nearly every evening she looked forward to stopping for a while at the Greater Salem Baptist Church on her way home. Regularly after she reached the bottom of the steps from the elevated station, she rushed to the church.

The church building was open almost every evening through the week. Many meetings were held, including social gatherings and the Wednesday evening prayer services. In addition, the church choir rehearsed several evenings.

During the choir rehearsals, Mahalia practiced singing both her solos and the songs she was supposed to sing with others. Also, she had to practice singing in special duets, trios, and quartets. Sometimes, when she wasn't practicing, she sang either by herself or with others just for the joy of singing.

Gradually, through her church activities, Mahalia built up a larger and larger circle of friends. She became so happy living in Chicago that she never once thought of going back to New Orleans to live. Someday, however, she hoped to go back for a visit.

In the early 1930's, soon after Mahalia became contented and happy, a great financial depression swept across the country. Banks failed, factories closed, and many workers lost their jobs. People lacked money to pay rent, buy food, and meet other expenses of living.

This depression was especially hard on the Negroes living in Chicago. They were among the first in the city to lose their jobs. Many had to find cheaper places to live, and others had to sell their automobiles and other belongings in order to get enough money to buy food. Some lost small savings in banks because most of the banks were closed.

Mahalia managed to keep her job but realized that something terrible was taking place. She knew little about the business world, however, and couldn't understand what was happening. Late one afternoon when she returned from work, she found a long line of men and women waiting in front of a bank. A big sign on the front door of the bank read, "Closed."

As Mahalia went by, she stopped to talk with some of the people. One woman, whose face was drenched with tears, said, "The bank has closed and I can't get in to draw out my savings."

"Well, you can draw them out when the bank opens," said Mahalia.

"What!" exclaimed a man. "This bank will never open. Her savings are gone."

"How can they be gone?" asked Mahalia. "If

she put money in savings in the bank, the bank is still saving her money, isn't it?"

"Oh, no," explained the man. "The bank paid out all the money it had and then closed its door. The rest of us have lost our money because of the depression."

Many of the women, and even some of the men, were crying. Some were trying to console one another by talking. Some were praying, "Oh, Lord, help us. We have lost both our savings and our jobs. What can we do?"

After Mahalia passed these sad and weeping people, she went on to the Greater Salem Baptist Church. When she stepped inside, she found another pitiful group of people. "I lost my job today," said a thin, neat-looking young man. "So did I," said another. "Lord come to our rescue," wailed several women.

Before long the depression hit Mahalia. She had to work longer hours and receive less money. Each afternoon when she returned home, she found people aimlessly walking the streets with no place to go. Some were begging to get a few pennies to buy a bite to eat.

After a few months, welfare agencies began to set up soup kitchens where they passed out free soup to hungry people. One cold, snowy winter afternoon, when Mahalia returned from work, she found a long line of people waiting outside a soup kitchen near her home. Most of them were shaking from standing for several hours in the cold wintry weather. Some prayed that the soup would last until they could go inside the building to get some.

Mahalia reached in her pocket and pulled out a wrinkled dollar bill and a few coins. She figured that she had enough money to purchase a few things at a grocery store. Then she called out to several nearby persons, "Come home with me and let me feed you."

Five or six adults and three or four halfgrown children followed her. She purchased some meat, potatoes, and vegetables, and cooked a big supper. The people thanked her tearfully, wondering when they would have an opportunity to eat a good meal again.

Mahalia's close friends in Chicago included Prince, Robert, and Wilbur Johnson, who were sons of the preacher at the Great Salem Baptist Church. During the depression these three young men, Mahalia, and another young lady named Louise Barry formed a quintet which they called the Johnson Gospel Singers. They sang regularly at the church and attracted wide attention. Soon people began to come from all over the south side to hear them sing.

Before long other churches on the south side, and later churches all over Chicago, invited them to come and put on concerts. In many cases they sang to help churches raise money.

During or after the concerts, the church officials took up collections. Then they took out part of the money for themselves and gave the rest to the members of the quintet. Sometimes the five singers earned as much as $1.50 apiece.

Later the Johnson Gospel Singers began to receive invitations to sing outside Chicago, in Illinois, Indiana, and Michigan. People liked their spirited, rhythmic singing because it helped them to forget their gloom over the depression. After each concert, persons usually gathered around to compliment them.

Several times as Mahalia traveled about with the quintet, people asked her whether she had ever taken singing lessons. One day she and one of her friends decided to take lessons from Professor Dubois, a noted Negro singer in Chicago. "Come in," said the professor graciously as they timidly entered his salon.

The professor talked with them briefly and

asked them to sing for him. First he took Mahalia to the piano and asked her to sing "Standing in the Need of Prayer." She started to sing in her usual spirited manner, but almost immediately he began to shake his head. Soon he held up his hand to stop her and said, "That is not the way to sing this song. Let me show you how."

The Professor sang the song in a much slower rhythm and far more softly than Mahalia had sung it. "Now sing the song again and try to sing it just as I've shown you," he said.

Mahalia clasped her hands in front of her, ready to sing again. At first she sang slowly and softly just as the Professor had shown her, but soon she bounced back into her old way of singing. "No, no, no," shouted the Professor. "You're ruining the song."

Next the Professor asked Mahalia's friend to sing the song. She sang it slowly and softly, the same as he had sung it for Mahalia. When she finished, he said, "That was beautiful. You sang the song just right."

The Professor now turned to Mahalia and said, "You shout too much when you sing. You'll have to cut out your shouting and learn to sing more softly and slowly."

Mahalia was greatly disappointed with this criticism and felt that her way of singing the song was better than the Professor's way. After they left the salon, Mahalia's friend said, "Wasn't Professor DuBois a fine teacher? I can hardly wait to return to take my next lesson."

Mahalia simply stared at her friend. "Well, I'm glad you were pleased, but I certainly don't want to learn his kind of music."

This was Mahalia's one and only singing lesson. She felt that singing came from the soul, not from following the whims of a teacher.

Mahalia Sings as a Soloist

ALL MEMBERS of the Johnson Gospel Singers held regular jobs. They had to work to earn a living because they didn't make enough from their singing. Often when they had an engagement to sing, only part of them could go. The others had to go to work on their jobs.

One evening when they had an appointment to sing at a church in Chicago, four of them had to work, and only Mahalia could go. When she arrived at the church, all by herself, the pastor was worried. "Where are the other members of your group?" he asked.

"They couldn't come because they had to go

to work," replied Mahalia. "I hope you won't object to my singing alone for your audience."

"Oh, no," replied the pastor nervously, "but I'll have to make an explanation to the people. We have announced that there would be five of you here to sing tonight."

Moments later the pastor led Mahalia up to the front of the church by the organ. "Ladies and gentlemen," he apologized to the audience, "I regret to announce that four members of the Johnson Gospel Singers had to work this evening and couldn't come to sing. The only member present is Mahalia Jackson, who will sing for us as a soloist this evening."

Mahalia stood by the organ, clasped her hands in front of her, and sang with all the strength and feeling possible. The members of the audience fell into the spirit of her singing and clapped their hands and stamped their feet to the rhythm. The pastor beamed with joy as

132

he listened to the music and watched the happy expressions on the faces of the audience.

After the concert, the church people crowded around Mahalia to praise her. "Your singing lifted me right up to the garden of paradise," exclaimed an old gray-haired lady.

"Yes, I could hardly keep from coming up here and singing right along with you," said a well-dressed man.

The news of Mahalia's singing spread, and she began to receive invitations to sing at other Negro churches on the south side. The pastor of one church after another said to her, "Won't you come to my church to sing?"

Mahalia liked to sing to Negroes because she felt they understood her singing. She sang in most of the Negro churches in Chicago, and soon began to sing in Negro churches in other cities. Within a few years she traveled throughout the entire country to sing. Night after night she sat up on trains to travel from one city or town to another. Often she stayed in a city or town for several days or weeks to sing night after night in the same church, or to sing in different churches.

One illustration of how she put on concerts is when she stepped off a train at a town in Missouri. She had agreed to sing at a church there for several evenings in succession. When she reached the station, the pastor was there to meet her. "Welcome, Miss Jackson," he said. "My wife and I have arranged for you to stay in our home while you are here."

As he escorted her along the streets from the station to his home, he told her much about his church. "My congregation includes some of the finest people in the world," he said. "They like music and are looking forward to hearing your good gospel singing."

When they reached the pastor's home, his

wife greeted Mahalia warmly. "Go into the bedroom with your things," she said, pointing to the open bedroom door. "After you wash up a bit, come on out to eat supper."

That evening, the pastor and his wife took Mahalia to the church to put on her first program. The church was packed with people who were eagerly waiting to see her and to hear her. Each person had paid a nickel admission to attend the program.

Mahalia sang four successive nights at the church, and each night more people came to hear her. On the last night they stood in the aisles and every available spot inside the church. Others stood outside and listened through the open windows and door.

When Mahalia started to sing, the whole church rocked to the rhythm of her singing. People in the audience clapped their hands and stamped their feet to the beat of gospel music.

Everybody was filled with the spirit of the Lord and wanted to demonstrate it.

Even though Mahalia traveled widely for gospel singing, she barely earned enough money to pay her expenses. Always between trips she tried to work to earn money. She had to give up her job as a laundress because she was away too much of the time. Later she obtained a job as a maid in a hotel, cleaning guest rooms. Occasionally she cleaned as many as thirty-three rooms a day. She worked at this job every day for two years, when she wasn't traveling.

Besides singing in churches, she occasionally sang at church conventions. At one convention, she was scheduled to sing with Professor Thomas A. Dorsey, a noted Negro composer of gospel songs. Two of his most popular gospel songs were "Precious Lord" and "Peace in the Valley," which had sold by the thousands.

Mahalia was proud to appear on the same program with Professor Dorsey and was eager to talk with him. "You surely have composed some mighty good gospel songs," she said. "How long have you been writing?"

"Ever since I was saved by the Lord," he replied seriously. "I started my musical career traveling about the country and playing the piano for Ma Rainey in her tent shows. In those days I was known as Georgia Tom."

"Yes," interrupted a man standing nearby. "Many people who went to Ma Rainey's shows still remember how you played that piano. You really made it come to life."

At once Mahalia thought about her father's cousins who once had come to New Orleans with Ma Rainey's show. She recalled how they had wanted her to travel about the country to sing in the show. "Did you happen to know Jeannette and Josie Burnette when you were in Ma Rainey's show?" she asked eagerly.

"Sure," he answered feelingly. "They put on a comedy act. We were in the same show."

Mahalia smiled. "Well, they were cousins of mine," she said. "Once when they came to New Orleans with Ma Rainey, they wanted me to go with them to sing in the show."

"I'm glad you didn't go," said the professor. "You don't belong in that kind of show. You're a gospel singer."

Even though gospel singers were popular, some preachers didn't approve of them. They were opposed to singing songs that led people to clap their hands and stamp their feet to keep time. They felt that such songs weren't dignified and should not be sung in a church.

One evening when Mahalia was singing gospel songs in a church, the preacher stopped her. "This kind of singing is not fitting in the house of the Lord," he exclaimed in an angry tone of voice. "You're just bringing jazz music into the

138

church. I don't want the members of my church to listen to such music."

These statements made Mahalia angry from head to foot. She stood erect and virtually shouted back to the preacher, "Reverend, I have read the Bible almost every day since I was a little girl. Let me call your attention to one of the Psalms, which reads as follows: 'Oh, clap your hands, all ye people! Shout unto the Lord with the voice of a trumpet!'" She started to sit down and then added, "You may not approve of gospel songs, but they're what the Lord wants me to go about singing."

One summer Mahalia's grandfather, whom she called Grandfather Paul, came from Louisiana to visit Aunt Hannah and Aunt Alice. Both Mahalia and her aunts were very happy to see him. One evening after dinner everybody sat around the table talking with him and asking him questions. Suddenly Mahalia looked over at him and wished that she had a picture of him for her room. "Grandfather," she said, "please have your picture taken while you are here."

Grandfather Paul smiled. "Who wants a picture of an old man like me?" he asked.

"I do," replied Mahalia. "Please have your picture taken for me."

"Who will pay for it?" asked her grandfather. "I can't spare the money."

"I will pay for it," said Mahalia.

Mahalia kept on teasing her grandfather, and finally he agreed to go to a studio. She gave him money to pay for having his picture taken, and he started out. The weather was warm and he had to walk for blocks in the hot sun. Then after he reached the studio, he suffered a stroke.

When Mahalia and Aunt Hannah heard this shocking news, they rushed to the studio in a taxicab. They found Grandfather Paul, motionless and barely breathing, stretched out on the

floor. Mahalia tried to talk with him, but he didn't even know she was there.

The photographer had already called an ambulance to come after him. Soon the ambulance came and took him into the emergency room at a hospital. Aunt Hannah and Mahalia waited anxiously in the hall for someone to tell them about him. Finally a doctor reported, "He's seriously ill and may not live through the night."

Aunt Hannah was almost overcome with grief. "Oh, how I wish you hadn't urged him to have his picture taken!" she said. "Then this terrible thing might not have happened."

Mahalia felt so guilty that she couldn't answer Aunt Hannah. She walked slowly down the hospital corridor until she came to an empty room. Sadly she went inside, fell on her knees, and prayed God to spare her grandfather. "Oh, God, forgive me for my selfishness," she said. "Please let Grandfather live."

She felt so guilty that she was eager to make some sort of sacrifice to save her grandfather. For years she had often dropped into theaters to enjoy motion pictures and vaudeville shows. "If you will let Grandfather live," she prayed, "I'll never go to a theater again."

Grandfather continued at the verge of death for several days. Then one day he started to get better, and Mahalia thanked God for saving him. Some days later she joyfully helped him leave the hospital and return to the apartment. There he recovered rapidly and soon was able to return to Louisiana.

Mahalia never went to a movie or vaudeville theater again. She felt that God had answered her prayers and that in return she owed it to Him never to break her promise.

Only Gospel
Singing

ONE EVENING at a social event, Mahalia met an attractive, well-mannered young man named Isaac Hockenhull. He had attended Fisk University and Tuskegee Institute in the South, where he had majored in chemistry. Following graduation, he had come to Chicago to look for a job. Most of his friends called him "Ike."

When Ike first came to Chicago, he had hoped to get a job where he could use his training in chemistry. He looked far and wide, but good jobs were scarce because of the depression. He kept up courage, however, and began to look for other jobs in which he could use his head as well as his hands. Finally he obtained a job as a mail carrier, but occasionally when there was little mail to carry, he was laid off.

From time to time Mahalia happened to see Ike again, and soon he began to ask her for dates. At first she hesitated to accept, because she felt so far beneath him in education. She couldn't understand why a man with a college education would want to associate with a young lady who never had gone beyond the eighth grade in school. Ike persisted, however, and she finally agreed to go out with him.

On their first date, she had very little to say. She was afraid that Ike wouldn't be interested in the simple things she would talk about. She hesitated to answer him when he said things to her because she didn't understand some of the words that he used. She actually was happy when the evening was over.

Ike liked to read, and often told Mahalia

things he had read in books. Now and then Mahalia had to stop him and ask what a word meant. One time she said, "Ike, you know too much for me. I can't even understand you when you try to explain things to me."

Ike laughed. "Well, maybe I know a few things that you don't know, including big words, but I can't sing as well as you can. In fact, I can scarcely sing at all."

"You don't have to sing, because you can do many other things," said Mahalia, "but I have to sing. Singing is about all I can do. Besides, I love to sing."

"Yes, but you are foolish to keep on with that gospel singing," said Ike. "With your voice you could go into show business and make big money. You could become a great artist and sing in theaters all over the world. Your name would appear in bright lights and you would meet important people, even kings and queens."

146

"No!" exclaimed Mahalia. "I'm not interested in that kind of singing. I just want to sing to please the Lord."

After nearly a year of courtship, Mahalia and Ike were married. At first they lived with Aunt Hannah, but soon moved into a small nearby apartment. Mahalia was especially happy because this was the first time she had ever had a real home of her own. Now, at last, she would be free to come and go as she pleased.

After her marriage, she kept on with her gospel singing and made frequent trips out of town. Between these trips, she continued to work as a maid at a hotel. She felt fortunate to have this job, but realized that sooner or later she would lose it because of her traveling. Every time she went on a trip, she had to ask other maids to take over her work.

After Ike was married, he tried to find a job to earn more money. He read want ads in newspapers and traveled about the city, trying to find a job where he could use his training in chemistry, but finally gave up. "I'll just have to keep on carrying mail," he said.

Always when Mahalia left on trips to sing, he was lonesome and wished she would forget singing and work steadily on her job at the hotel. Several times he pointed out that she would make more money by working steadily. If she still wanted to sing, he urged her to get a job singing in Chicago.

Ike was very proud of Mahalia's singing, but he had no feeling for gospel music. He couldn't understand why people clapped their hands or stamped their feet when she sang. To him music was an art, in which singers stood on stages in theaters and sang to vast audiences. Besides, they were paid good money for singing.

From time to time when Ike had a few days off from carrying mail, he wished he had some-

148

thing to sell. One day he decided that by spending a few dollars, he could make some cosmetics to sell. Once his mother had made and sold cosmetics in St. Louis which she had called "Madame Hockenhull's Cosmetics."

Ike still had a few bottles and jars of his mother's cosmetics, which he promptly got out and examined. He decided to use the same name for his cosmetics and to follow the same formulas in making them.

He went out to a drug store and purchased all the necessary ingredients. Also he bought numerous bottles and jars which he spread out on the table. That evening he began to measure and mix the ingredients to make the different lotions and creams. Since he had training in chemistry, he knew exactly what to do.

Mahalia was interested in Ike's new venture and tried to help him all she could. She washed and polished his bottles and jars and arranged them neatly on the table. When he finished preparing a sweet-smelling lotion, she poured it into some of the bottles. When he completed a cream, she dipped it out with a wooden paddle to fill some of the jars.

They worked on and on, determined not to stop until they finished filling the bottles and jars. They were so interested that they lost all track of time. Occasionally Mahalia became sleepy, but she wouldn't give up. Finally early the next morning, they stood back and proudly looked at the table loaded down with bottles and jars of Madame Hockenhull's Cosmetics.

During the coming weeks, Ike went to nearby stores and shops, trying to get the owners to agree to sell his cosmetics. He stopped at houses and apartments, trying to sell lotions and creams directly to women in their homes. Money was still scarce and he met with little success, but he kept trying.

For a while he encouraged Mahalia to try to sell his cosmetics. He figured that while she was traveling about the country, she could sell lotions and creams to audiences. "People will be glad to buy from you," he said.

Mahalia was eager to help him and managed to sell quite a number of bottles and jars. People were still poor from the depression, however, and only a few could buy.

Soon Ike came to realize that his cosmetics business was doomed to failure. He not only had trouble selling his cosmetics, but he couldn't spare money to keep on making them. He needed his money for other things.

About this time Louis Armstrong brought his band to Chicago to appear at a leading theater. While he was there, he hunted up Mahalia and invited her to sing with his band. "I want you to sing the blues with us," he said. "You can start immediately and set your own salary."

"No," replied Mahalia. "I don't get the least bit of joy out of singing the blues, but when I sing gospel songs, I get thrilled through and through. That's my kind of singing."

Ike was greatly annoyed with Mahalia for refusing to accept this job with Louis Armstrong. He couldn't understand why she would turn down an opportunity to sing with one of the most famous bands in the country. Further, he couldn't understand why she would turn down an opportunity to earn big money for singing. To him she was wasting her time singing gospel songs for little or no money.

At last he decided to have a heart-to-heart talk with her. "I'm afraid my life is doomed to failure," he said sadly. "When I graduated from college, I thought I could conquer the world. I came to Chicago with high hopes of getting a good job, but the depression wiped out most of the good jobs for Negroes. Then I tried to start that cosmetics business, but couldn't make it go. Actually right now I guess I'm lucky to have my job as a mail carrier."

"Don't be discouraged," said Mahalia.

"You're an intelligent, ambitious, well-meaning young man who deserves a better opportunity."

"But I'm fast losing my ambition," said Ike soberly. "I haven't anything to count on in the future, but you have your voice. I wish I could persuade you to quit that gospel singing and to start singing for money. You just turned down a wonderful offer to sing in Louis Armstrong's band. Well, if you don't want to go into show business, why don't you take a few singing lessons and become a concert artist? With your voice, you could become one of the greatest concert artists in the world."

At the mention of taking singing lessons, Mahalia threw up her hands. She thought of the time when she had planned to take singing lessons from Professor DuBois. She vividly recalled how he had told her that she did too much shouting when she sang. "Oh, no," she exclaimed to Ike. "Please don't ask me to take singing lessons.

154

Once when Professor DuBois tried to show me how to sing a song, I felt as if he were trying to strangle me. I just have to sing from my heart in my own way."

Once more Ike gave up arguing. He went on carrying mail, and Mahalia went on traveling to do gospel singing. Nearly every day he combed want ads in newspapers and applied for jobs but couldn't find anything better.

Once when Mahalia came back from a long singing trip, she found that he had lost his job as mail carrier. He had spent nearly all their money to pay the rent and to buy food. "Don't worry," said Mahalia. "I'll stay at home for a while and work steadily at the hotel until we catch up on funds."

Mahalia was in for a great disappointment. When she went back to the hotel, she found that she had lost her job, too. Slowly she walked back home to break the sad news to Ike.

Together they spread out and counted all their money. Mahalia sadly paced the floor, and Ike sat slouched forward in a chair with his face in his hands. "Oh, what shall we do?" asked Mahalia. "What shall we do?"

"You'll just have to start singing for money," replied Ike. "There's no other way."

Mahalia was torn with anguish. On the one hand, she felt guilty of letting Ike down. On the other hand, she felt that she just couldn't sing for money. "I just can't," she said.

Singing
My Own Way

MAHALIA AND IKE had just finished breakfast
and Ike began to look at the morning newspaper.
Soon he cut out a clipping and handed it to
Mahalia. "Look at this," he said. "Here is a real
opportunity for you."

The clipping explained that auditions were
being held to select a young lady to sing the
leading part in a famous show called *The Mikado*. Mahalia read the clipping carefully and
said, "Oh, no, I don't want a part in that show,
or any other show. I just want to keep on singing
gospel songs."

"You can get that part just by going over and

singing for the judges," he persisted. "Then you will be started on a famous career. You'll travel all over the country and sing to thousands and thousands of people."

Mahalia sat quietly and held her head between her hands. She realized that somehow she and Ike had to find jobs to earn money, but she just couldn't bring herself to enter show business. Painfully she kept holding her head and saying, "No, no, no."

Ike now became very angry. He jumped up from his chair and shouted, "I don't see how you can just sit there and shake your head. Here's an opportunity for you to become a great artist. God gave you a special voice for singing. Now why don't you use it?"

"I am already using it," cried Mahalia. "I'm using it to sing gospels for God."

Following this statement by Mahalia, Ike grabbed his coat and hat and started to leave.

158

"Well, I'm going out to look for a job," he said coldly, "and you had better do the same."

Mahalia watched sadly as he left and felt guilty for not going out to look for a job, too. With great hesitation, she read the clipping which he had left on the table. It explained that tryouts for the show were being held at the Great Northern Theater.

Slowly she arose from the table and put on her coat. She patted down her hair but didn't even glance in the mirror to see how it looked. Mechanically she picked up the newspaper clipping and boarded a streetcar, which would take her downtown.

When she reached the theater, she scarcely could muster enough strength to go inside. She felt as if she was about to do something wrong. "May I help you?" asked a woman at the door.

"Oh," replied Mahalia, still in a daze, "I came for an audition to *The Mikado*."

"Where is your music?" asked the woman. "You'll need something familiar to sing."

Mahalia reached in her purse and counted the few coins she had left. Half-heartedly she walked down the street to a music store. There, much to her surprise, she found a copy of the old Negro spiritual "Sometimes I Feel Like a Motherless Child." She purchased the copy and started slowly back to the theater.

This time the woman at the door took her to the audition room. The man in charge wrote down her name and the title of her song. He told her to take a seat in the back of the room and wait until he called her name.

One after another, the man called off the names of the contestants. Each time a young lady went down front and stood near the piano to sing her chosen song. If the judges liked her singing, they let her sing a complete song, but if they didn't, they stopped her soon after she started. All the while Mahalia hoped that a young lady would win before her turn came to sing. Suddenly she heard the man call out her name, "Mahalia Jackson."

At once she felt cold and clammy. She arose and walked slowly down front to the piano. Hesitatingly she handed the music to the pianist, who took it and started to play.

During the next few moments she stood stiffly with her hands at her sides, waiting for the pianist to play the introduction. Unfortunately, however, since she couldn't read music, she couldn't tell when to start singing. The pianist looked up at her in disgust and played the piece right to the end. Then he started to play the introduction again.

This time Mahalia could tell when to start. She clasped her hands, closed her eyes, and sang feelingly, as if she were the real motherless child in the song. Everybody in the audition room looked at her in wonder and was entranced by her singing. The judges smiled and nodded their heads in approval.

As soon as Mahalia finished singing, she walked back to her seat and picked up her coat. She could tell that she had sung well, but she was eager to leave before the judges could tell her that she had won. She still didn't want the part and was eager to escape.

For some time she walked the streets to try to get control of herself. At last she boarded a streetcar and rode back home. When she arrived, Ike was there waiting for her. He threw his arms around her and shouted, "You've won! I knew you would if you would only try!"

Ike whirled her round and round without giving her a chance to take off her coat. "The judges just called to report that you have won!" he shouted. "They want you to start rehearsing your part tomorrow. This is your lucky day. At

162

last you're on your way to both fame and money. Nothing can stop you now."

After this reception, Mahalia sank wearly into a chair. She didn't know what to say or do. Tears came to her eyes. Soon she asked, "How did you come out in looking for a job today? Did you have any luck?"

Ike stopped cold. "Yes, I got a job, but not what I wanted," he replied. "I'll make about as much as I did before. Of course, my job can't compare with yours."

"Please give me a chance to think," said Mahalia, starting to take off her coat. "Right now I'm all confused."

"But you haven't any time to think," said Ike. "Everything is settled and you're supposed to start rehearsing tomorrow."

Mahalia went into the bedroom to hang up her coat. She realized that she faced making one of the most crucial decisions of her life, and that she must make it immediately. She sat down on the edge of the bed to read a few comforting passages from the Bible. Finally she dropped on her knees beside the bed and prayed, "God, please give me strength and guidance. What shall I do about this matter?"

Soon things began to shape up in her mind and she felt that without question she must say, "No." She must not allow herself to be swayed by the thoughts of singing either for fame or for money. She must sing only for God.

Bravely she climbed to her feet and went out to tell Ike. "I'm sorry, Ike, but I just can't accept that offer to sing in *The Mikado*," she said. "That's not my kind of singing."

From then on her marriage with Ike was never the same. Gradually as she continued her gospel singing, they began to lead separate lives. Always, however, they remained close friends.

Eventually Mahalia began to worry about

what to do if she had to give up gospel singing. She decided that she should be able to fall back on some other way of earning a living, if necessary. Finally in 1939, she attended a beauty school and started a beauty shop, which she called "Mahalia's Beauty Salon." A short time later, she opened a flower shop, which she called "Mahalia's House of Flowers."

From the beginning she proved to be a very successful business woman. She hired good workers and was eager to please her customers. She tried to supervise both her shops and to meet as many persons as possible. Usually she spent her weekdays in Chicago and traveled over the weekends to do her gospel singing.

Both the beauty salon and the flower shop became very popular on the south side of Chicago. Women were proud to have their hair done at Mahalia's Beauty Salon. People purchased many flowers at Mahalia's House of Flowers for weddings and funerals. Often when a family purchased flowers for a funeral, Mahalia offered to sing at the services.

After Mahalia did less traveling to sing, she began to make records of some of her gospel songs. Her records became popular, because many persons now could enjoy her singing who never had an opportunity to hear her sing in person. Also, many persons who heard her sing in person wanted to buy her records. Soon music stores throughout the country began to advertise and sell her records.

During this period World War II was in progress and many homes were broken with young men away in service. Mahalia's gospel singing was especially comforting to these families, especially Negro families. Somehow her singing gave them a new spirit of hope.

One day a woman named Bess Burman, from Apollo Records, happened to hear Mahalia sing an old spiritual, "Movin' on Up." Miss Burman had never heard the spiritual before, but decided at once that it would make a good record. "How long have you been singing it?" she asked.

"All my life," replied Mahalia. "Tonight I sang it just as I did down in New Orleans."

"Well, you certainly sang it just right," said Miss Burman. "Now I hope you'll agree to make a record of it for me."

In 1946, Mahalia recorded this spiritual. Within a few weeks it began to sell so fast that music stores couldn't keep it in stock.

Sudden Rise
to World Fame

AFTER MAHALIA began to make records, she became more and more popular as a singer. At first her popularity was limited largely to Negroes, but gradually it came to include many white people. From time to time she was invited to sing to all-white audiences.

As Mahalia's popularity increased, many persons wanted to find out more about her kind of singing. In many ways she seemed to differ from most popular singers. She sang largely gospel songs in churches, but others sang either jazz and blues songs in night clubs and theaters or sang opera songs in huge halls.

People were curious about how she learned to sing. They couldn't believe that a person with her ability had never attended a music school or taken singing lessons. Some even felt that without such training she couldn't possibly be a talented singer.

Gradually music colleges and special music groups became curious about her singing. They wanted to study it somehow, to find out what made it so popular. Finally they began to invite her to come to meet with them so they could study her type of singing. Some hoped to get valuable ideas from her to include in their training courses.

Usually when she visited a college, she first sang a few songs and afterwards the students and professors bombarded her with questions. "How did you get started to sing?" asked a student at one of the colleges.

"I don't know," replied Mahalia. "My father

170

was a preacher of a small church down in New Orleans. When I was a little girl, I went to his church and sang with everybody else. I guess singing was part of growing up with me."

"Why do you sing only gospel songs?" asked another student.

"Mainly because they're what I first learned to sing," replied Mahalia. "They're closer to me, and I love to sing them. Down in my heart I feel they're what God wants me to sing."

"Without training, how do you know when to sing softly or loudly, or when to sing fast or slowly?" asked still another student.

"I just depend on my feelings to tell me," replied Mahalia. "When I sing, I try to make people understand me just as I do in talking."

"Don't you ever feel a need for taking singing lessons?" asked a professor.

"No, I don't need lessons for my kind of singing," replied Mahalia. "I sing from my heart for the glory of God. Lessons might even hold me back in my type of singing."

"Don't you ever have an urge to sing on the stage or in a show or to become a concert singer?" asked another professor.

"No, I've had opportunities to go into other types of singing, but I have turned them down," replied Mahalia. "I have no desire to sing for fame or money. My only ambition is to sing well for the Lord."

Most of the colleges which Mahalia visited were Negro or mixed Negro and white. In 1950, she was invited to sing at an all-white conference of music professors to be held at Music Inn in the Berkshire Mountains of Massachusetts. The purpose of this conference was to study and discuss folk music and jazz. Music professors from all the leading colleges of music in the northeastern part of the country were invited to attend the conference.

The meeting was called by Marshall Stearns, Professor of Music at the New School for Social Research in New York. He had heard Mahalia sing a number of times and was interested in her gospel singing. He wanted her to sing some of her gospel songs and answer questions for the group. This invitation to meet with the group of white professors came as a great surprise to her, but if they wanted her, she was glad to accept.

When Mahalia arrived for the conference, Professor Stearns explained that the sleeping quarters were still under construction and that everybody had to sleep in temporary quarters. He picked up her traveling bag and escorted her to an old barn where she was to sleep. After he left, she started to laugh and said, "Well, I finally made it to the white folks' world, but I have to sleep in a barn."

After Mahalia and the professors finished eating supper, Professor Stearns asked Mahalia to sing a few songs. In response, she stood by a piano and sang "Jesus Savior, Pilot Me," "Didn't It Rain, Lord," and "Movin' on Up."

When she finished singing, the professors loudly clapped their hands, but remained speechless. They were stunned by the beauty of her singing and could think of nothing to say. Then all of them broke loose at once and started to ask questions. "Where did you go to college?" "Where did you take singing lessons?" "How did you learn to sing with such strength and feeling?"

The questions came so rapidly that Mahalia couldn't possibly answer them. At last Professor Stearns waved his hands and asked the professors to give her a chance to talk. She explained that she had learned to sing as a mere child by attending a Baptist Church in New Orleans. "I never attended college, and I never have taken

174

a singing lesson," she said. "I just sing the way I feel God wants me to sing."

Afterwards the professors asked Mahalia to sing more songs so that they could make some recordings. When she finished, they praised her for the way she controlled her tones. "Your control is almost perfect," they said.

Mahalia laughed at their comments. "When I sing, I just breathe and let the tones come out. For me music comes from the soul. I just sing and forget everything else."

The next morning when Mahalia awoke in her makeshift room in the barn, she was surprised to hear tape recordings of her own voice. Some of the professors were already playing recordings of the songs she had sung the night before. She shook her head, wondering why they were so curious about her singing.

She stayed at the conference for a full week, singing and answering questions. The professors wanted to find out as much as possible about Negro church music. They wanted to know how Negro gospel songs got started. They wanted to know why Negroes seemed to have a special fondness for singing the blues.

At one of the last sessions Mahalia sang "Shall We Gather at the River?" After she finished singing, one of the professors grabbed her hand to congratulate her. "If you had started to walk down to the river while you were singing," he said, "all of us would have followed you right down to the water."

When Mahalia returned to Chicago from the conference, the whole world was clamoring at her door. She received an invitation to appear on the Ed Sullivan television show, one of the leading talent shows in the country. Also, she received an invitation to put on a concert at Carnegie Hall in New York, where only the finest musicians are invited to appear.

Mahalia's concert at Carnegie Hall broke all attendance records. When she walked out on the stage, there was only a small space next to the piano for her to stand. All the seats in the hall and even special seats on the stage had been sold. Most of the audience was composed of Negroes from all over the East.

As Mahalia stood on the stage before this throng, she felt timid and fearful. She realized that she was standing on the same stage where great artists like Lily Pons and Marian Anderson had already appeared. After she started to sing, however, she gained confidence and sang with unusual spirit and charm.

Following this successful appearance, she was invited to make a concert tour of Europe. She hesitated to accept, because she was afraid the Europeans might not understand or enjoy her gospel type of singing. Finally she made a tour of Belgium, Holland, Denmark, and France, where she was greeted by large and enthusiastic audiences in all countries.

She was thrilled with her acceptance abroad but found her tour extremely tiring. Near the end of the tour, she became so exhausted that she had to spend most of each day in bed. Her accompanist, Mildred Falls, and others tried to get her to give up the rest of the tour and return to America, but she refused.

At last, despite her persistence, her tour abruptly ended one night in France. She had spent the day in bed and when evening came she could scarcely muster enough strength to attempt to put on a concert, but she insisted. "These people have bought seats and are counting on me," she said. "I can't let them down."

That night when Mrs. Falls played the introductory music, she kept wondering whether Mahalia could possibly walk out onto the stage. Promptly at the proper moment, Mahalia, dressed in a black velvet gown, gracefully walked onto the stage, ready to start singing. She sang gloriously throughout the concert and the audience went wild with enthusiasm.

Nobody at the concert realized that she was ill, but afterward she collapsed and had to be flown back to Chicago for a major operation. Gradually she recovered but had to cut down on her strenuous activities for a while. Much of the time while she was ill, she spent planning things that she wanted to do in the future.

At this stage she was highly pleased with her wide acceptance as a singer. She was especially pleased by how well she had been accepted among white people. "I only hope that from now on I can be accepted to the same extent as a person," she said with a smile.

Busy Final Years

AFTER MAHALIA recovered from her illness, she was invited to put on a radio show in Chicago, which soon was converted into a television show. One half hour each week she sang religious songs, mainly by herself but sometimes with guests. Many people wrote her letters to tell her how much they liked her show.

Her show was so popular that people in other parts of the country began to clamor for her to put on a national television show. One day she discussed the matter with some of the executives in the television studio where she put on her program. The executives listened politely, but shook their heads and said, "You can readily get a sponsor for your television show here in Chicago, but you couldn't possibly get a sponsor for a national hookup. Too much prejudice still exists against Negroes in certain parts of the country."

Mahalia was stunned. She hadn't realized that so much prejudice against Negroes still existed. At first she had sung only to Negro audiences, but now she was singing to many white people, even to all-white audiences. Besides, she couldn't understand why singing religious songs should offend anybody.

Already she had appeared as a guest star on several national television shows, including those of Ed Sullivan, Steve Allen, Bing Crosby, and Dinah Shore. She knew of other Negro guest stars who had appeared on these and other national television shows. She couldn't understand why she wouldn't be allowed to have a national television show of her own. "Yes, I'm a Negro," she said, "but I don't understand why being a Negro should keep me from having a national hookup."

Mahalia found out in several other ways that prejudices still existed against Negroes. Occasionally she and her accompanist, Mildred Falls, traveled by automobile to put on programs in other parts of the country. Often her cousin, John Stevens, a young actor and drama teacher in Chicago, served as her chauffeur. Now and then when they arrived in a city or town, they were not allowed to register at a hotel or to eat in a restaurant. In some places they found signs reading, "No Negroes allowed."

In most cities and towns, white persons attended Mahalia's program along with Negroes. They applauded her enthusiastically and often came forward to tell her how much they enjoyed her singing. As soon as she stepped outside, however, she found herself in an entirely different sort of world.

One year her long-time friends and relatives invited her to sing at a Christmas program at the Mount Moriah Baptist Church in New Orleans. Shortly after she had accepted this invitation, Dave Garroway invited her to appear on a national television program on Christmas. "I'm sorry, but I can't accept," she explained. "I have already promised to sing at the Mount Moriah Baptist Church in New Orleans."

"That's all right," replied Garroway. "Just go ahead with your plans and we'll televise you from the church."

Mahalia proceeded to arrange a program. On Christmas she and her relatives and friends gathered at the Mount Moriah Baptist Church and sang together just as they had when she was a little girl. Two of their numbers were "Born in Bethlehem" and "Sweet Little Jesus Boy," which ten million persons in the television audience thoroughly enjoyed.

Through the years Mahalia became a close friend of Martin Luther King, Jr., and Ralph Abernathy of the Southern Christian Leadership Conference. Once they invited her to sing at a rally in Montgomery, Alabama, to help raise money to promote the equal rights movement for Negroes. Mahalia accepted and sang to an overflow crowd.

After this trip to Montgomery, Reverend King and many other Negro religious leaders often visited Mahalia in Chicago. She was pleased to work with them in their efforts to bring about acceptance of Negroes as American citizens. She was especially eager for Negroes to have opportunities to become hard-working and deeply religious persons.

Mahalia always took particular pleasure in encouraging talented young Negroes. She wanted

them to feel that they could succeed if they would only believe in themselves. "Once the Lord took hold of me and picked me up," she said. "He will do the same for you."

Soon Mahalia was invited to put on a concert at Constitution Hall in Washington, D.C., to help break down racial prejudices. Both Negroes and white people attended the concert in the spirit of brotherly love. They clapped and shouted with joy as Mahalia sang some of her soul-searching songs.

In January, 1961, when John F. Kennedy was inaugurated President, he invited Mahalia to sing "The Star Spangled Banner" at the inaugural ball. Surrounded by some of the greatest celebrities in the country and world, she sang our national anthem with unusual fervor and pride. To her, the American flag was the greatest flag in the world.

Later the same year Mahalia made another

triumphant tour of Europe. She was greeted by audiences that clapped and hollered for more. In Hamburg, Germany, the audience kept on cheering after she finished and wouldn't let her go. Finally she came back on stage in her street dress and sang two final songs.

At the end of this successful European tour, she went on to visit the Holy Land in western Asia. To her, this visit seemed like the fulfillment of a dream. "At last I've seen where Christ was born and have touched the Rock of Calvary," she said.

From the Holy Land, she went to Tel Aviv, the capital of Israel. Here she sang a series of religious songs expressing deep faith in God, including "I Found the Answer," "He Got the Whole World in His Hands," and "When the Saints Come Marching In." When she concluded by singing "Joshua Fit the Battle of Jericho," the audience rocked with the rhythm of her singing.

In August, 1963, Martin Luther King, Jr., invited her to sing at a great civil rights meeting in Washington, D.C., known as the March on Washington for Jobs and Freedom. Over one hundred thousand persons interested in civil rights traveled to Washington to hold meetings and urge Congress to pass laws to give Negroes equal voting rights with white people in America. The people set up tents in the parks and spent several days in the city.

One day during the session Mahalia was scheduled to sing and Reverend King to speak from the steps of the Lincoln Memorial. Tens of thousands of persons gathered on the plaza in front of the Memorial to hear them. When Reverend King introduced Mahalia, she stood beside him and sang an old Negro spiritual entitled "I Been 'Buked."

At first she sang the lines softly and then repeated them in regular gospel rhythm, clap-

189

ping her hands as she sang. Thousands of persons in the audience joined in clapping and the whole plaza rocked with rhythm.

In his address Mahalia heard Reverend King thrill the crowd with his famous words, "I have a dream." Then he went to on say:

> "This will be the day when all of God's children will be able to sing with new meaning, 'My Country 'Tis of Thee, sweet land of liberty, of thee I sing.'"

Through the years Mahalia was invited several times to sing at Carnegie Hall and other famous halls in the country. Each time she sang with deep emotion and just let the music come out. Her tones ranged all the way from low whispers to loud shrill notes. Always she maintained a touching rhythm.

Mahalia, who was born in 1911, came from a lowly home along the Mississippi River in New Orleans. She was raised by a deeply religious aunt, who regularly took her to church. The pastor of the church was her own father. Here she developed a fondness for gospel singing that lasted throughout her life.

She completed only the first eight grades in school and never attended a music school or took music lessons. She never even learned to read music, but felt that singing came from the soul with the help of the Lord.

After she became known, she had many opportunities to go into show business or to become a concert singer, but she insisted that she never wanted to sing for fame or for money. She felt that she should sing only for God.

Even though she could not read music and had no desire to become famous, she became one of the most popular singers in the world. She sang before hundreds of thousands of people in person and to hundreds of millions on records, radio, and television.

She always was proud to be a Negro, and she worked hard to improve everyday living conditions for Negroes. Through her singing she became an important civil rights leader. She appeared on many programs to help break down racial prejudices in America.

Mahalia Jackson died in Chicago, January 27, 1972, but her gospel singing will live long after her. She always felt that gospel music meant the bringing of good tidings and the spreading of good news. She felt that gospel singing was the only kind of true music in the world because it reflected deep faith in God.